A Stag from Rum

AN ESSAY IN POACHING

Robert Atkinson

THE ISLANDS BOOK TRUST
Urras Leabhraichean nan Eilean
LIVING HISTORY

Published in 2015 by the Islands Book Trust

www.theislandsbooktrust.com

© Islands Book Trust 2015

ISBN: 978-1-907443-65-7

Text © the Estate of Robert Atkinson

Islands Book Trust
Laxay Hall
Laxay
Isle of Lewis
HS2 9PJ
Tel: 01851 830316

Typeset by Raspberry Creative Type

Front cover image by John and Jan Fisher of Fisher Studio and Gallery, Pittenweem

Printed and bound by Martins the Printers, Berwick-upon-Tweed

The publisher's sincere thanks go to the School of Scottish Studies, Edinburgh, the curators of the Robert Atkinson archive; namely Dr Cathlin Macaulay and Colin Gately, who between them provided the material for this work and transformed yellowing contact prints into sharp digital images. We are especially grateful to John and Jan Fisher of Fisher Studio and Gallery, Pittenweem for the inspired and striking cover picture, which captures perfectly the spirit of the story and to Peter Holt who undertook the necessary and usually unsung task of proof reading. Our gratitude also to Robert's children, Ed Atkinson, Tom Atkinson and Sally Dakin for their permission to publish the manuscript and their unstinting support in the process of doing so; and finally to Donnie Morrison for many hours spent on the OCR capture of the text.

Contents

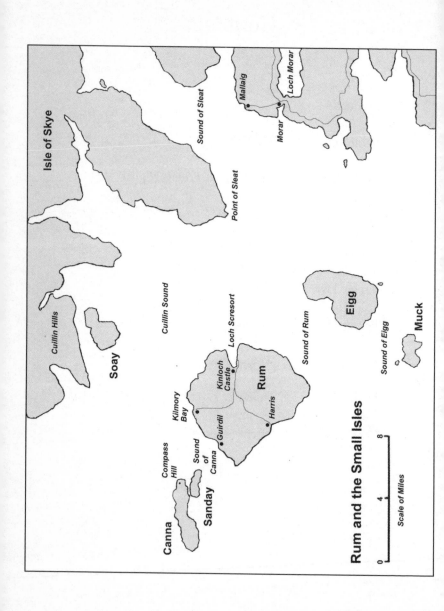

Rum and the Small Isles

Isle of Skye

Cullin Hills

Soay

Cullin Sound

Sound of Sleat

Point of Sleat

Mallaig

Morar

Loch Morar

Canna

Compass Hill

Sanday

Sound of Canna

Kilmory Bay

Guirdil

Kinloch Castle

Loch Scresort

Rum

Harris

Sound of Rum

Eigg

Sound of Eigg

Muck

0   4   8

Scale of Miles

Introduction

Published here for the first time, from a rediscovered manuscript, *A Stag from Rum* is a true tale of poaching and youthful *joie de vivre*. Robert Atkinson noted the story in his diary during the few days in August 1938, when the escapade took place. As it amounted to a detailed confession of a crime that would have implicated his fellow poachers, Hugh LeLacheur and John Naish, discretion at the time seemed the wisest course. Only long afterwards did he approach a publisher, but the manuscript was rejected and subsequently lay unread for the next 30 years.

The idea of being 'John Macnab' came from John Buchan's story of the same name, in which three disaffected aristocrats, finding running the country not challenging enough, turn to poaching to alleviate their boredom. Under the collective name of 'John Macnab' they go undercover in the Highlands and challenge neighbouring estates to try and stop them poaching on their ground. Although the inspiration for taking a stag came from Buchan, Robert was also outraged by Rum's forbidding reputation at the time, the estate actively discouraging people from landing. He was determined to protest that by at least a flamboyant act of trespass.

Rum had a well-earned reputation for not being a welcoming place and throughout the 19th century the island had suffered under a succession of ill-tempered autocrats who treated the people with appalling thoughtlessness. In 1826, the first and worst, Dr Lachlan MacLean forced the emigration of nearly the entire native population of 350 souls; two years later he finished the job by 'assisting' the passage of fifty more. Rum was cleared of its native Gaelic people and the link between people and place was broken. It never recovered from that single, brutal event.

By the time John Bullough bought the island in 1888 the population was about seventy. Bullough was a millionaire Lancashire mill owner who intended to turn the island into his personal sporting paradise, but he died three years later. His eldest son and heir George Bullough took up those ambitions on a grandiose scale. This was epitomized by Kinloch Castle, completed in 1901 – an enduring monument to Edwardian style and one man's personal extravagance. The Rum of the Bulloughs gained its reputation for over-indulgence in the years up to 1914: the yachts, the parties, the lavish hospitality of the stalking season, the risqué behaviour of its wealthy and titled guests. Whether true or not, the passing of time has embellished the antics on Rum. No doubt the isolation of the island fostered exaggerations, but it was little different to what was going on across highland Scotland at the time.

The island's heyday was long past by 1938, with even the population at an all-time low, down to only thirty or so, including the few children in the school. The adults were employees of the estate and all were living in or near Kinloch. In one capacity or another the worker's day would have focused on Kinloch Castle and the policies. As the stalking season and Sir George's annual pilgrimage drew closer they would likely have busied themselves getting the place ship-shape, so would have little reason or inclination to be roaming the hill ground. When he did arrive, off the mail boat *Lochmor*, the days of private steam yachts being long over, the entire staff would have made themselves conspicuous to welcome the laird to his island. So, in an ironic twist of coincidence, as Sir George arrived on that 16th August in 1938, and while the head stalker and under keepers were doffing their bonnets to the laird, over the hill the latter day 'John Macnab' was making off with one of his stags, a fine eight-pointer.

Of course, since the three poachers were neither caught nor confessed, their deed hardly amounted to any sort of protest about access rights. Rather, what they did was successfully take a stag and thereby commit a crime. Had they been caught, the estate would not have been amused, for the typical Scottish landowner's view of poachers was that 'hanging was too good for 'em' and nothing much has changed in that regard.

Still, had they wanted to make things easier for themselves they could have done so by shooting on a mainland estate. Their chances of being caught there would have been negligible, unless, like 'John Macnab', they threw down the gauntlet beforehand. On Rum that would have guaranteed them being caught, but by choosing to go there at all it could be said they met the challenge halfway. There were also other difficulties. They had no recent intelligence about the island and could hardly give the game away by asking Mallaig locals for the information they needed to plan the campaign; for example, on the number of inhabitants, who lived where, how many gamekeepers there were and when the laird would be in residence. It was a stroke of luck that Sir George only arrived in the week of the attempt; had they been a week later stalking parties would have been active on the hills and a rifle shot unlikely to pass undetected.

Indeed, luck was with them all through the escapade. So much could have gone wrong. When something did, like the boat sinking into the sand at the limit of high tide, they would have been scuppered but for the cargo of pit props washed ashore nearby that enabled them to lever the boat free.

Once away from Rum they faced getting back to Mallaig, in a dangerous following sea. Of course, they had no survival equipment: radios, flares, inflatable dinghy, lifejackets or the like. If the worst had happened and the boat had broached, they would either have had to cling to the wreck, if she stayed afloat, or swim for the nearest shore. Turning back to shelter wasn't an option, so their coolness in continuing took not just luck, but judgment, steady nerves and real sailing skill, especially by John Naish, to bring them safely into port.

The three protagonists who were briefly 'John Macnab'; Robert Atkinson, Hugh LeLacheur and John Naish, had one characteristic in common with Buchan's fictional Macnabs – boundless self-confidence. However, the one main difference was that Buchan's Macnabs were in weary middle age, while Atkinson & Co were in the prime of defiant youth. Hugh, Robert's cousin, was the youngest at twenty. Robert and John, who had been at university together, were both twenty-three. All had still to make their mark, but only John, studying medicine, had decided on a career. Another shared trait was these young men's love of boats and the sea; all three proved to be natural born seamen.

When war came in 1939 all three were called up from the start, since they were already in the RNVR, the Royal Naval Volunteer Reserve. John Naish had become Dr Naish and was posted to the tropics for the first two years, finishing up in Ceylon. Posted back to England, he spent the remaining war years in Portsmouth, leaving the navy in 1946. Hugh

LeLacheur was not to survive; his battleship *HMS Barham* was torpedoed in the Mediterranean and sank with enormous loss of life. He was just twenty-three years old. Robert had what we would now call a 'hot war', although it started relatively quietly on armed trawlers escorting convoys from Scotland. In 1941 he was posted to motor gun-boats operating in the English Channel and eventually rose to command one of these, during which time he was 'mentioned in dispatches,' the definition of which is 'gallant or meritorious action in the face of the enemy'. This occurred during the disastrous Dieppe raid in 1942. Both the gun-boat's then commander and another officer were taken prisoner in a desperate attempt to rescue troops from the beaches, which suggests they must have been in the thick of the action and lucky not to have been sunk or damaged. Even so, Robert made it through unscathed and left the navy in 1945.

It was during the war years that Robert began writing both *A Stag from Rum* and *Island Going;* the latter a book that has rarely been out of print since its publication in 1949. It is now regarded as a classic of travel writing – perceptive and gently humorous in its depiction of the islands and their people. He wrote then that he 'should never regret the devotion (to the Hebrides) of the precious first five summers of my twenties'. They were the years from 1935, when he and John Ainslie first came to the Highlands looking for a way to North Rona, the remotest of all the Hebrides. Rona was achieved in 1936. Thereafter Robert returned to the islands every summer, broadening his experience and gaining new friends. The last year, 1939, just days before war was declared, saw him buy the *Heather,* an old but sturdy wooden fishing boat. This was the way forward, the means to do just as he pleased in future summers, and he and Hugh were in enthusiastic agreement about the possibilities. So the *Heather's* first voyage was the last epic of those years, sailing her round from Loch Roag on the west coast of Lewis to Stornoway and nearly sinking on the way, saved by a passing herring drifter which towed them in. This was Hugh's only voyage on *Heather* and his last adventure in the islands; as Robert expressed it in *Island Going*, Hugh was left behind in 1941.

With the war over Robert wasted no time in returning to the Hebrides and in 1946 took *Heather* out for her first proper sea voyage, a return to North Rona, ten years almost to the day since his first, month-long stay with John Ainslie. Then they had been complete innocents in the ways of the islands, focused on unravelling the breeding cycle of the rare and little known Leach's fork-tailed Petrel and eager for the pleasures of a month alone on a deserted island. They came back now to familiar places and renewed island friendships and Robert at least continued his Hebridean summers. Some part of these years is described in *Shillay and the Seals* (1980) but after his marriage and, with growing family commitments, the long summers in the islands gradually dwindled, finally ending with the tragically early death of his wife and the need to support his three growing children.

Robert never fully lost touch with the Hebrides but after his last visit in 1969 he never returned. However, his book *Island Going* struck a chord with a younger generation who were eager to share their island experiences with him; ever hospitable, he was happy to hear their stories and encourage their enthusiasm. A modest man, he only gradually became aware that what he had done in documenting parts of his life had a worthwhile, historic value that deserved to be properly archived. In particular, his meticulously catalogued collection of Hebridean photographs, showing the islands in the 1930s and 40s, have proved especially useful for archaeologists documenting the slow decay of human artefacts on St Kilda and North Rona. This collection of negatives and prints he gifted to the School of Scottish Studies in Edinburgh in 1985, where it has been widely used to illustrate a range of academic publications. Likewise, his war diaries and photographs have been sent to the Royal Naval archive in Greenwich and *Island Going,* his memoir of a well-spent youth, remains in print and continues to win new admirers.

As for the 'Stag', it is now published as a story worth telling for its own sake and as a tribute to Robert and his fellow bold spirits, Hugh LeLacheur and John Naish, who successfully brought the fictional 'John Macnab' to life on the forbidden hills of Rum.

Stuart Murray

Chapter One

Location

Mallaig is not quite what you would expect; but then what would you expect of a West Highland railhead placed rather over a hundred miles from the north end of Scotland and backed by coastal mountains? Of course blind imagination could never supply all the detail, but surely you could get the general atmosphere. This is the raw material: West coast railhead reached by a single track line winding through fifty miles of Buchan country; steep bare rock, burns and lochs, midges, hanging birch slopes, place names in the Altnaharra tradition; fifty miles from Fort William at Mallaig.

Well, for a start, there would be a station. A chill empty waiting room of course, but it would be of highland stone, squat, with fuchsia bushes beside it. Some nearly leafless raspberry canes, wind-rattled against a wooden paling? Or old and woody blackcurrants, entirely barren and with salt-browned leaves? One of the bleached telegraph poles would have clasped to it a posting box whose red paint would be lustreless as rust. A Scottish fatherly old porter, naturally. A bare stretch of platform, its sleepers scrubbed light by weathering; the enclosed wooden fence would be white painted, with diamond-pointed pales.

Mallaig is none of that. It is extraordinary how the 'railwayness' of the station remains inviolate; the station has a roof that helps to keep its atmosphere together. So a tourist, urban and nostalgic, returning from the train-less Western Isles, might sniff and say "Ha," and think himself home again. The western swell beating against the rocks a few yards from the train, the lash of salty rain, the cries of the gulls, dour herring driftermen – surely they leaven the 'railwayness' so thickly concentrated within the station? But it is not so. The Mallaig branch of the London & North Eastern Railway remains, within its dingy compass, the perfect abstraction of any large railway station anywhere; it is almost a caricature. Porters' greasy caps, trollies with loose iron wheels, unlikely posters, stale chocolate machines, sleepers impregnated with black oil – there they all are.

Outside the station it is usually raining and the potholes in the street are turbid. The street leads from the station past one or two shops to the head of the fish quay. It then divides. The main thoroughfare turns sharply away from the water, goes up like the roof of a house past the post office, a couple of low bars and the West Highland hotel, and disappears into its inland switchback. The other road follows round the brim of the harbour and is lined with houses, the residential quarter; at the far end the new raw brick jerry-builts are clustered. They are obvious and incongruous from seaward, being apparently set down indifferently on the bare stone or rough grassed hillside. Except along the few paces of main street, buildings are everywhere terraced out of the hillside. The fall of ground is so steep that the town always seems to be roofs, seen through a screen of telegraph wires, of which there are many. Its

Scottish importance calls Mallaig a town, for a great volume of the Mainland – Western Isles traffic and goods passes through it; but in England it would be a small, unprepossessing village. The population is of a few hundred, sufficiently few to be looked after by a single policeman who, in the way of the force in Scotland, is very human. The three or four shops are of the village emporia class: postcards and groceries, oranges, fishermen's oilskins, wrapped bread. They style themselves 'General Merchants'.

The wooden huts of the fishcurers' offices are on the quay. This is an area of railway lines much dotted with those uniquely railway-ish embossed, cast iron notice boards about company's liabilities and vehicular traffic. Shell and Esso, the paraffin trollies, are as brightly painted as a pillar box. They are backed up to the edge of the quay, and feed down to the fishing boats made fast alongside. The fishing boats are a long way down at low tide, unmoving in the slack water whose oily film and harbour rubbish barely pulse to the tide; while outside there may be a hearty swell running white against the rock in the mouth of the harbour, where the iron cage stands.

Into Mallaig come MacBrayne's steamers, *Lochness*, *Lochmor*, *Lochearn* and the rest. The *Lochness* is on the Stornoway run, up to Kyle and across to Stornoway in the day, and back again at night. The others work variously the Inner Isles, Small Isles and the Outer Isles mail routes. Trains from Glasgow meet the steamers and steamers meet the trains. There is a great bustle of friends and relations, commercial travellers, holiday makers, extraordinarily dressed hikers from Glasgow bound for Portree in Skye, baggagemen and officials, all being rained on. The importance of being Mallaig.

The volume of traffic through Mallaig reaches it by rail and sea; but there is also the road, which is by way of being notorious. It is lightly said to be the worst 'A' road in the British Isles. Many motorists decide not to use their cars along it, and many more say they wouldn't have, if they had known. It cannot be said to be anything of a feat to traverse the road because the importance of Mallaig often makes the use of it obligatory. But that does not detract from its reputation. In the same way there are issues of the weekly motoring papers with no mention of the Mallaig route, but this can only be due to editorial realisation that variety is the spice of life. As a subject of conversation the Mallaig road comes easily to hand. You could not drive a car for long in the Outer Isles without being asked whether you shipped at Mallaig or Kyle (repetition of Mallaig further up the coast but with a new chromium plated railway hotel, without fishing and served by a good road). It was Mallaig? The subject is opened at once. If you are in Scotland with a car and meet a motorist who has done the road, you will soon know it; now hear of its outcrops of bare rock, its loose scree slopes, spacious potholes and hilltops of the sort that rear a car's bonnet skywards to blank off the driver's view of the other side of the crest. I have met a man who told me how on that road he had stripped off one of the back wheels of his big F--d – clean sheared the studs. I never care to miss an opportunity of abusing F--ds. When a driver takes the road slowly he can feel the whip of the car's frame and when he tires of the slow jolts, and accelerates, the car simply judders. If bad patches on fairly level, fairly straight pieces of track are taken really fast, at 25 or even 30 mph, the car continually leaves the ground, to crab and bounce when it lands. The remains of cars that have failed to make the grade are to be seen abandoned by the roadside. There was once an old Bentley that knocked its sump off against one of the rock outcrops; but then those old Bentleys have very little ground clearance under the engine.

The road is not really so bad. The chief cause of its notoriety is its status as a main road, an 'A' route joining Mallaig to Fort William. Personally I have clocked one hour fifty minutes dead for the fifty miles, an extraordinary time, which necessitated the style of driving in which all four wheels leave the ground together. This was in the early morning when there was no traffic. Attempts on this time should only be made in a very old car. Mine was ten years old and received a bruising from which it did not readily recover. It is now juddering out the last of its days on the roads of the Outer Isles, in the hands of a Lewis lorry driver to whom I sold it. He was delighted with his £5 bargain and I in turn was pleased with my good price.

The Mallaig road is now under imaginative reconstruction and in a few years will be a first class highway; but not so exciting as in the old days. Meantime, blasting operations often strew the track with boulders which block the way for a time, unless the driver gets out to set an example to Gaelic nonchalance. A great amount of heavy machinery has been gathered by the road. Flint crushers, air compressors, pneumatic drills and heavy lorries are deployed in those highlands and army huts accommodate the road gangs. There are also the skeletons of lorries, worn out at their work, then discarded to the ditch. There are even steam rollers, monstrous fish out of water; in that context one would be equally surprised to meet a giraffe. The mind boggles at the idea of their having wheezed their way from Fort William by road, but how else could they have gained the highland scene?

New bridges, cuttings through the living rock, corners short circuited, embankments lifting the road across valleys;

the new Mallaig road will be smooth, fast and straight. Then watch the local motor cycles and, no less, see the venerable vans of the General Merchants take a new lease of life.

Chapter Two

Time
(up to Friday night)

At 8 o'clock in the morning I woke up on the deck of the steamer, feeling cold, evil and cramped, to see just the black arm of a crane against the sky. I knew it at once for the Mallaig crane. The steamer was the *Lochness*. The morning was a Saturday in the middle of August. The *Lochness* had crossed from Stornoway during the night and had put in at Kyle at about 4 am; the shivery dawn. A time when sleep on the uncovered deck is most precious, yet not to be preserved through the loud noises of the steam winch three paces away from your head.

I had been in the Outer Isles with a friend who had gone back early and he had left me to bring his car home. It had been a bird expedition, with red-necked phalaropes in North Uist as the chief joy. After he had gone home I had parked his car in the garage attached to the Tarbert Hotel in Harris, and had gone off alone to various remote places. On the way back the steamer had to stop especially for me off Rodel, where a motor boat, warned by wireless and with some complication, was lying off in wait. Stopping the

14

steamer costs five shillings extra, a pleasing tariff. Rodel is in the extreme south of Harris, which, at its northern end, abuts Lewis along a land boundary. Lewis and Harris are jointly one big island, the largest, most northerly and most important of the long line of the Outer Isles. At 3 o'clock in the night an old, old bus had left this place Rodel to clatter inland and northward, its poorly lights a little moving island in the black land of bog and stone. The Rodel – Tarbert road is one of the worst highways in the Outer Isles and is of the Mallaig tradition. Buses have to meet the mail boats whose timetables, even if kept, bring them to the island piers at all hours. This particular bus, with me on board, had reached Tarbert at about 4.30 am and on this occasion had found the steamer lying at the pier another little island of light and activity in all the sour darkness. I had not had any sleep since I don't know when. The hotel had been open too, to receive any rich English fishermen from London via Glasgow and Mallaig, thence to the Outer Isles mail boat route to Tarbert, as the timetables have it. I had collected the car, driven north through the Harris mountains into Lewis; and into Stornoway at 6.30 am, when a red sun was just clear of the horizon and steam drifters were gliding in across the mirrored, early morning stillness of the harbour water, to the deserted town.

That Stornoway morning was a Wednesday and was followed after an interval of two days, by the Mallaig Saturday morning previously described. From the Wednesday to the Friday evening I had enjoyed, for their own sakes, the familiar novelties of hot baths, a bed with sheets, dry, clean clothes and food prepared by another's hand. Then, after so short an interval of homely comforts, I had started again the accustomed irregularities, and had begun with the Friday night spent huddled on the uninviting deck of the *Lochness*.

15

The point in arriving in Mallaig on that Saturday morning was not only because it was on the way home (although I did not go on straightaway to Fort William and the south, a 24 hour drive); it was because Mallaig was the chosen rendezvous. Three of us had arranged to foregather there. This was our purpose: to obtain a boat, to sail westward to the island deer forest of Rum and from those mountain reserves, to take a stag.

That project, which we thought to work out from the Mallaig rendezvous, is the thesis of this essay. With imaginative embellishments and some repressions and alterations, I daresay it could be made into quite an exciting story. It would then lose, as I see it, its *raison d'etre*; that of being a practical experience, but that makes it sound important, which I never believed. The detail, incidentally, is not invented; memory has enlarged it from a rough diary kept at the time. Nowadays you cannot plan forwards, you can only recall and the writing up has been pleasant recollection; the slim volume is of an evening's retrospect.

The project then, and Mallaig. I was apparently about to meet the rest of the personnel. This is premature, however – although I hoped Hugh and John were already on their way north – because a lot of preparation and thought had already gone before, and might now be retraced.

An idea such as the Rum project, being lightly conceived, illegal and suggestively kith to an undergraduate frolic, is of the class of idea that is almost invariably stillborn. When the idea came to me I thought it practically certain to die a natural. I knew some of the Isles fairly well; I had been on both Canna and Eigg which bracket Rum from the north and south. So I knew about Rum and had heard some of the many stories and rumours which surrounded it. Irresistibly, these stories bred the idea. The relevant fact was simply that Rum was an island given over entirely to deer forest, on which landing for any purpose whatsoever was absolutely forbidden.

Many of the stories made play with the strategies of people who had been determined to land, and that for no other purpose than the satisfaction of stepping on forbidden ground. I know that yachtsmen who enter Loch Scresort on the east side of Rum, to try the freshwater excuse for landing, get no satisfaction; their dinghies are kept off by keepers or other minions. I know one yachtsman whose burly crew equalled in number the defence squad and they landed in defiance – "you're not stopping us from getting freshwater and if any of you so much as lay a finger on that boat," etc – they got the water they did not want, and left again, dogged, but, by force of numbers, unmolested. You can buy a steamer ticket to Rum but you must stay aboard the steamer. I have heard, but I don't know if it has any truth, that once a shipwrecked crew was turned away from Rum. The island, in its inhospitality, is very different from any other islands I know, or of which I have heard tell, where the rule is free for all and a most kindly treatment.

One liked to think that behind the screen of prohibition and taboo, Rum hid some secret or subversive activity. But what? What could be guarded in the steep and mist-covered hinterland? Fuller's earth, gold, or even the goose which lays the golden eggs; the directing intelligence, the secret headquarters, of an international crime gang; death ray laboratories; German submarine base; the Philosopher's Stone. Any of these would have answered well. But apparently it was only deer and all the fence of restriction was to preserve them so that they might live undisturbed until they were required to be shot; but exclusively at the invitation of the proprietor.

Given this knowledge of Rum and its deer, the project was easily born. It would be a gesture. Its apostrophe would

17

be: 'You think you can shut off a large island for the exclusive use of a few rich old men? For the exclusive purpose, and that during only a short season, of shooting a few wild cattle? Devote a British island eight miles by six to a wilderness of deer? Deny access to anybody and everybody lest the precious deer be scared for five minutes? Damned cheek. Our gesture will be to obtain a boat, land, and remove one of your precious stags.'

John Macnab – the title of one of Lord Tweedsmuir's Scottish books – at once came to mind. We got a copy to read again. For our purpose this book was simply the story of how J Macnab sent a challenge to the owner of a deer forest. He, Macnab, declared that he would take a stag from the owner's preserves, between such and such times and he defied whatever forces the owner might bring forth to stop him. We read it on the lookout for practical hints. But our expedition would naturally not go advertising its intentions with challenges; or for that matter, with handsome contributions to any named charity if it failed, in the Macnab style. There is no doubt that his way was much the more sporting and he, of course, never dragged in social injustice as an excuse. But it was going to be quite difficult enough for us to reach even the stage of an unobserved landing on Rum. Thereafter, if we got so far, we should have a likelier chance than John Macnab had, in that we should be unexpected; but a far lesser chance in that:

(1.) The deer forest was an island and you could not run for it if you were caught.

(2.) None of us knew anything about deer stalking.

The plan was first mooted nearly a year before the August Saturday morning in Mallaig of which I am writing. Of the three of us concerned Hugh was keenest; certainly without

18

him the idea would have faded out, as I thought all along it was bound to do. He was working in the City and would have a fortnight's holiday. He would devote half of this to Rum, he said. John was the third. He had not qualified, and was still a student at a London hospital; we had been at Cambridge together – all the old stuff. He was good with boats and would be in charge of the Rum boat. Hugh and I would do any shooting. Supposing, which I did not, that the enterprise ever came off, I thought we would probably either slink about the mountains of Rum without seeing any sign of stags, be unable to sail at all because of bad weather, or be unable to hire a boat. We discussed many airy plans, most of which were impractical. Given the Rum project to carry out, what strategy could be constructed in advance?

Our early plans were elaborate and story book. Landing parties and boat parties were adumbrated: systems of signals from shore to boat, comings and goings at dead of night; early morning stalks, remote rendezvous for boat and stalkers to reunite. That sort of thing was soon discarded. A boat of the size that could lie off at sea and could carry a dinghy for landing would take two or three people to handle, and was altogether outside the scale of our plans. In any case there were only three of us. We should have to rely on a boat small enough to pull up on a beach and that meant calm weather. John, alone, could not cruise a boat about indefinitely while Hugh and I went stalking. The party would have to keep together and pull its boat up on shore. In those waters you cannot anchor a boat and leave it to look after itself. Nor, unless you are a native of those parts, can you land at night or sail after dark near the rocky coast. It appeared that little in the way of practical plans could be made from London. The boat would have to be hired in Mallaig and I did not know whether there were any boats for hire there, or, if there were, whether we should find something suitable for our purposes. A seaworthy dinghy with an outboard motor – something about twelve or fourteen feet and good and beamy – was our provisional idea of a suitable boat.

Mallaig, the only possible point of Mainland, is twenty miles from Rum. I had seen those waters, the Sound of Sleat and the Sea of the Hebrides, as calm as a millpond, calm enough to show an undisturbed reflection of each floating gull. But dinghy weather is rare thereabouts, even in summer. I believe there must be more days when it is impossible to cross even to Skye in a small rowing boat, than days when a crossing is possible during the average summer. We should have to depend entirely on the luck of good weather and it would be required to hold while we sailed the twenty miles to Rum, found a landing at some point of its rock-bound and unpleasant coast, attempted to discharge our business and sailed twenty miles back.

I said none of us knew anything about deer stalking. This certainly, could not be planned from London. The little we found out about it seemed to show that it was very difficult, and that nearly all the credit of a successful stalk was due to the professional stalker who knew his ground. If we located stags on Rum, to get on terms with them we should have to trust only to common sense; but of this, naturally, we assumed our due. The actual shooting would probably be the easiest of all, should the enterprise ever reach that stage. Getting to Rum and getting in range of a stag would be the real problems. The resident personnel of Rum, minions of the chase, were an unknown quantity; they had to be disregarded in any long term planning. So had the proprietor.

Through winter and spring the Rum idea still drifted along, being booked for execution some time in August.

But, as far as I was concerned, the early keenness and anticipation had been eclipsed. Our daring gesture, I could not help thinking, would be, if it fruited, no more than a silly undergraduate-ish prank and underhand and deceitful at that. I had no particular wish to kill a stag, whoever it belonged to. And if other people with plenty of money did, that was no doubt their own business, even if it extended to the inhospitable and unnecessarily severe closing of an entire island. No doubt they would trot out the old story that it kept people in employment who would otherwise be unemployed. We could not afford to come into the open with a challenge. What the hell is the good of a gesture if nobody knows anything about it? On the other hand it would be a tremendous satisfaction to take, somehow, a stag from a closely preserved island deer forest; there were, undeniably, romantic points there. A reflection that contradicted the taste of deceit was that good poaching is never found out and perfect poaching is never so much as suspected, even after the act. This plan necessitated the premise that the adjective 'deceitful' is inapplicable to poaching; and so be it.

At the beginning of July the idea was still extant. Later in July I left for Scotland upon my lawful occasions, and went about the Outer Isles as mentioned before. That was the time of the locating of a breeding ground of the so rare and diminutive red-necked phalarope. The Rum arrangements had been left in the air, except that Hugh was to get hold of a rifle. When I got back to Stornoway I would tell Hugh so by telegram. He would then announce his holiday, leave the office forthwith, collect John and drive north. Meanwhile I would be crossing to the Mainland by the mail boat. We should all meet in Mallaig.

When I left for Scotland I reckoned I saw clearly what would happen to the Rum expedition. It had to be pinned

21

down to one single week, date not yet decided. We should all meet in Mallaig, and when at the end of the week the weather had still not eased off, we should disperse and go home. So much for preamble. Now, to go back to Mallaig and before that, to the Wednesday morning on which at 6.30 am I had just arrived in Stornoway.

As soon as the post office opened I telegraphed Hugh that I was back, and asked him to ring me up that evening. He finally got through just before midnight and we had six minutes, the line being then at its best. Hugh said that John had disappeared; he, Hugh, had written to him at his flat and had had no reply. He had rung up the flat and been told that John had gone to Anglesey for five weeks. Hugh said he would telegraph him that he was to be collected from Anglesey on Saturday. They would try to arrive in Mallaig on Sunday, Hugh said. Yes, he had got hold of a rifle.

Thursday

Telegraph from me to John in Anglesey:

> HUGH ARRANGING TRANSPORT YOU MALLAIG THIS SATURDAY CAN YOU MANAGE THIS ESSENTIAL YOU TELEGRAPH YES HELL OF JOB CHASING AFTER YOU ROBERT.

Friday

A bad thunderstorm over Thursday night and Friday early morning put the landline across to Skye out of action. (It always was a weak link, but now the GPO has installed radio- telephony across the Minch) This notice was put up in the Stornoway post office: 'Post Office Telegraphs. NOTICE OF DELAY. There will be ... heavy ... delay in the transmission of telegrams to ... The Mainland, N. Uist, Barra etc ... in consequence of ... extensive lightning damage.

22

By order of the Post-Master General.' But the line was open for a time in the morning and let through a telegram for me:

HOPE TO ARRIVE MALLAIG WITH JOHN HUGH.

After this the line was either up or down again, but was open later on. Another telegram came through:

COMING WITH HUGH STOP JOHN.

Priority telegram from me to Hugh:

THANKS MUCH RELIEVED STOP JOHN ALSO CONFIRMED STOP WISH YOU JOY OF MALLAIG ROAD ROBERT.

At 11 pm the *Lochness* left Stornoway and arrived at Mallaig at eight next morning; that Saturday morning which is continually being mentioned. Once and for all I got off the boat.

Chapter Three

Saturday

The friend's car which had been left to me to bring home was slung ashore. I drove it over the railway lines, past the embossed iron notices, into the hub of Mallaig. There was nothing for me from the others at the post office. The Marine Hotel overlooks the station roof and is reached by a flight of steps in the rock, which thus outcrops even in the main street. At the top of the steps I looked out west through the screen of telegraph wires, over the station roof and all across the wide water to the Small Isles. The morning had opened to one of those enormous blue and white Hebridean days. The low battleship shape of Eigg lay on the horizon. Another island was beside it in the sun and cloud shadows. Its roof just touched the cloud layer. In Mallaig the sun was obscured, but over the water the island was mountain-blue and there were gentle slashes of greeny detail where sunlight struck between the cloud shadows. It was Rum, of course. The expedition seemed anything but underhand with its destination standing there so large and open.

I booked a room in the hotel and asked for breakfast. Now I came to think of it I was lucky to find a room in one of the only two hotels, seeing that it was mid-August and Mallaig full of visitors, either resident or coming and going to and from Skye. I was given an attic room, lined with varnished matchboarding in the traditional Scottish style, and giving on to the harbour. There were some small smart yachts at anchor or at mooring. The lavatory overlooked Eigg, over a different sector of telegraph wire and gull-splashed roofing. I could not crane out far enough to see Rum as the window would open just so far and no more, true to its type. Breakfast was very crowded with trippers and kippers which made me, with my secret purpose, feel objectionably superior. There was not room to read a book. The neighbours on either side of me finished their breakfasts, paused and said uncomfortably: "Please excuse me". Oh dear, I had quite forgotten the rules of hotel behaviour; I was not playing up at all.

A friend in Stornoway, Mr MacX, had sent a telegram on my behalf to Mr MacY in Mallaig, who is a prominent native and who might be able to put me in the way of a suitable boat. Like all Mr MacX's telegrams this one was written as spoken, with a fine disregard for the extravagance of 'ands' and 'tos'. Mr MacY I found to be one of the General Merchants. He stood behind his counter, stout and benevolent; his black alpaca jacket was not supposed to encompass his waistcoat. I mentioned Mr MacX's telegram and he slowly took off his spectacles, produced the telegram, and came out through the flap in the counter to shake me by the hand. We discussed the question of a boat. We wouldn't be going far, I said, and admitted that we did not intend to sleep on board, but to go ashore and camp. I tried to be vague – a cruise around the Isles for a few days – and when pressed said the names of Eigg or possibly Canna. But Mr MacY went on about Rum and how landing was forbidden. I shrank inside. There were several people in the shop and Mr MacY spoke out very plainly. In our telegram we had carefully referred to Rum as George, going to see George. I hastily reassured him but he would go on about Rum, and loudly, bold as brass. The island was particularly forbidden now, because of the shooting. He hadn't seen Sir - - , he was the owner you know, go through yet. He didn't think he would have missed him. He believed he would be coming through Mallaig on Tuesday (in three days' time that made it.)

This was awful, and so openly said. I got him off the subject eventually, feeling rather disturbed; it was not a good beginning. But I was glad to hear that about the movements of the owner. All I knew of the personnel of Rum was that there were no crofters but plenty of keepers, stalkers, ghillies and suchlike, and the castle servants; altogether an intimidating tribe, no doubt. I had heard Sir - - mentioned recently as the owner of Rum; I think casually mentioned in a conversation about Skye shepherds' complaints about golden eagles coming over from Rum. The shepherds were displeased that the eagles' numbers were not kept in check. The owner, of course, was no concern of ours – at least we sincerely hoped it wouldn't be – but I was sorry to have to hear his actual name, and also the circumstance that he was only a seasonal visitor. Rather I had fancied a picture of a crusty and unapproachable laird, a permanent inhabitant feared by all and defying all comers. I would have much preferred never to have known his name or anything at all about him as it would have been happier (and easier on the conscience) if he could have remained a mythical character of my imagination. This business about Tuesday though, that was a nice piece of chance information, and might be of practical value. Suppose we went ashore on Tuesday? Perhaps the keepers would be gathered to greet their laird? What extraordinary

26

luck if we could then have the run of the unpatrolled, unwatched policies, if that was what they were called.

Mr MacY asked me if I knew the Isles and I said airily, "Oh yes". I realised he meant us to hire a boat with a man attached. He would be able to find us one on that condition; there was another thing not allowed for. It would be far more difficult to hire a boat without a man, said Mr MacY. There were no outboard motors in Mallaig, only inboards. He would see what he could do, however, during the day.

I wandered about Mallaig, commenting unfavourably to myself on what I saw, in the English way, and enjoying the various spectacles offered by the place. There were several motor boats in the harbour. The ones I saw were too big and heavy and narrow – motor launches rather than motor boats, useless to us whether they were for hire or not. Nor could we rely on sail alone, knowing nothing of those waters, but more particularly because of the time factor, because we must be able to go where we wanted when we wanted. More likely that would be contrary to winds and tides and would call for a well-found motor.

I saw that the travelling cinema had visited Mallaig the previous night, but only for the one night. It had passed on, perhaps to Portree in Skye, or else back along the road to Arisaig. I was sorry to have missed this social force. The shop windows displayed Scotch Broth tinned by Heinz and this was a pleasing observation. It is always interesting to look through the Highlands and Islands telephone directory; a page or two covers the subscribers of all the Isles. Mallaig holiday people were largely Glasgow tourists, but there was a sprinkling of English and Scottish gentlefolk, some kilted. I felt uncomfortable near these and kept away. The name of the motor launch plying as ferry between Skye and Mallaig is the *Ossianic*. I had always ignorantly supposed this to be an advertiser's spelling of 'oceanic', supporting the thesis of Americano-Daily Express degeneration spreading to the Western Isles. The Express has a Scottish edition of course. But *MV Ossianic* merely 'pertains to Ossian' and is thus the uncontaminated Celtic.

The two hotels which offer themselves to the Mallaig visitor make a difficult choice. The AA, a poor guide in any case, mentions neither. I have summed up some of the points which should be taken into consideration.

The Royal West Highland, lately the Station, is certainly Mallaig's leading hotel, but it has that atmosphere of sniffy sanctity so common amongst leading hotels; this may date from its change of name. Against this the Marine is, well, jolly, and certainly more suitable cover for our expedition as it is easy to be inconspicuous in the amorphous throng. The Marine fails badly in being dry. West Highland coffee is naturally far better, and is served in two silver pots. The Marine's comes ready mixed, of unknown origin, in one pot, but of silver nevertheless. The Marine now scores an unexpected point as it is the West Highland's grapefruit which comes out of a tin and the Marine's is served as nature made it. The breakfast prices are the same – 3/6 – the customary Scottish overcharge, so the choice resolves into coffee v grapefruit, the rest being equal.

In the evening I behaved nicely at the Marine dinner, with polite conversation to make up for being unshaven, and remembered the punctilios of leaving. Incidentally, most Scottish hotels deal only in breakfast, lunch – pardon, luncheon – and high tea; dinner is usually a monopoly of the most classy. After this I went to see Mr MacY again. He would think he could get a boat on Monday, but definite arrangements should wait until then. The Scottish Sunday operates strongly in Mallaig. Mr MacY took me to the owner of the proposed boat.

He was a young man, smart in the Burton style, who had made good by cornering, as I gathered, lobster distribution from Mallaig. He mentioned something about a Kelvin sleeve valve, which sounded too important for us. It was agreed to leave the matter until Monday morning as we would not be able to start until then anyway. By then the rest of the personnel should have assembled and have had a chance to ventilate their newest plans and opinions and to have censured my inefficiency I suppose.

I would say here that having been alone for some time I had had too much opportunity for reflection on the moral issues involved; the risks and the probable penalties for a miscarriage of fortune. I would be glad when it was all over. Being alone, my chief relief was that I hadn't to undertake Rum on my own; it would be alright when we all got together. I looked forward to hearing English voices again, to meeting the others and not caring a damn for anyone.

Too much reflection also vouchsafed to me that this was the first time I had deliberately set out to break a fairly important law. Previous minor defaults were not in the same class at all but were commonplace only: licence for what could, I suppose, be called a wireless set; gun licence; car tax expired but risked it; an odd pheasant here and there, and so forth. Offences re deer, I discovered, are governed by laws framed when deer-poaching, or, as it is bluntly called, deer-stealing, was naughtier than it now is. I found £50 mentioned as a penalty. I decided I would prefer to do time; in the Fort Willie's jail, that would probably be.

Supposing that something did go wrong, the circumstances would no doubt cause a lot of painful publicity. The Buchan tie-up would ensure that, itself unlikely to go unremarked. (There would be a short note appended

29

to the court press report, summarising the story of *John Macnab* for the benefit of readers not acquainted with the work.) The defence, pleading levity, could only be on the humiliating grounds of 'boyish prank'; but the obvious premeditation, particularly the hire of a rifle, would count against this. The responsibility was mine, I felt, however much the other two had repudiated this earlier on. If we were caught, I knew very clearly that it would not be us who would be most damaged, but our elders. A brush with the police would not upset me personally, though indeed for John as nearly a doctor or for Hugh in the City it would be extremely unfortunate. The idea of even sharing in responsibility for such misfortune, and more so for the upset to others not of the party, was unpleasant.

As instigator (or just recipient – it came unbidden) of the Rum idea, the first person I had told of the circumstances concerning the island was Hugh and at once, from that data, he had brought forth exactly the same idea. When my enthusiasm had cooled, I took the unedifying line: 'well I think it's a bloody silly undertaking but, as you're still keen, I suppose we'd better get on with it.' Unenthusiastic preparation, as once for the beginning of term, was the spirit.

All this has been brought out merely to demonstrate that the actual risks are the least of the many worries of law breaking. That is, of law breaking on any scale larger than commonplace Government cheating; the Government, in minor differences, being usually considered fair game.

These responsibility worries were much more important than conscience. The disquiet of conscience, I decided, was easy, and was not concerned with law breaking. It was simply that I did not like feeling in the wrong. If the idea

30

had been, say, to plant a flag on the highest and most forbidden peak of Rum, conscience would never have stirred, however much trespassers might be prosecuted. One is brought up with such regard for property that I found that conscience questioned the desirability of stealing somebody else's stag. All the same, I always plead difficulty in believing that a wild animal can belong to anyone.

Talk of responsibility was not allowed by Hugh and it angered him to hear it. John was not so concerned at all, having been invited in as O/C Boats. He expected, no doubt, to arrive in Mallaig to find everything taped and he would not be pleased to find even the boat not yet forthcoming. I had taken the view that, definite planning being impossible from London, 'It Would Be All Right on the Night'. But now, having come first to Mallaig and being the only one who had visited the place before, I felt I had not much to offer. I was doing it wrong. I should have stayed in Arisaig. The hirers of the boat should have appeared from the unknown. As it was we should infallibly leave traces all over Mallaig. Making a getaway from Rum but being seen in the process was the worst danger. Rum is on the telephone. Possible evidence left on Rum to be followed up by the authorities made it essential that the trail be impossible to pick up on the Mainland. As it was nothing could be easier. The police would be neither baffled nor unable to find a clue.

But now it was Saturday night. We had had the excitement, however childish, of telegrams and plans and phone calls from one end of the British Isles to the other. Now of the three, one had arrived and the other two were converging on the rendezvous from London and the Welsh Coast. I did not care if I was old enough to know better, nor did I care that an expensive education had inculcated no greater reverence for private property.

'Doin' the Lambeth Walk' had at this time penetrated the Western Highlands, the Outer Isles and, probably even the Small Isles; but with the exception I considered, of Rum, and possibly Muck. It was rendered now outside my Mallaig window.

Chapter Four

Sunday

As I said before, the weather would be the key point. It would decide whether or not we should get even to the stage of setting out from Mallaig. So the prefatory weather was of some moment although, in my experience, forecasts more than one day ahead for the West Coast are impossible. The natives are unlike those of any other part of the British Isles, they do not readily volunteer even the shortest term forecast. Often I have asked what the weather was going to do and have only been answered with an uninterested, "couldna say I'm shoor". Anyway, up to the end of July that Scottish summer had been awful, with strong winds, cold, big seas and sheeting rain. Then a quick change gave a hot, flat, muggy serenity to the first ten days of August. The open Atlantic was then an oily calm, slow-heaving with a low, hardly visible swell. On some of those days you could have landed at the cliff base on the west coast of the Outer Isles, something which is probably impossible throughout a normal run of years. For the next week the weather was less settled but still mainly fine and reasonably calm, though showing suspicions of breaking-up. The end of that week was the Mallaig Saturday.

Now, on Sunday morning, the sun was hot from a blue sky whose white clouds had no hint of grey. A light breeze came off the sea.

I got the car out, drove it a mile or two out of Mallaig and pulled off the road at a place where it was nearly at sea-level, skirting the head of a sandy bay. The west was all blue water, the sun was hot from the south and the breeze warm. The air and the waves moved in from the west, the latter tiny on the rippled sand because the rocks and their slow-swirling weed had taken the power from the tide. The little waves were practically raised by the breeze across the lake of the bay, like freshwater waves. I unloaded the car, putting together one or two things I should want on Rum, looking up at the sound of every occasional car approaching from the far side of the next rise. The small continuous sounds of breeze and tiny waves made a Sunday silence. The lassitude, as of English high summer, was helped by the bluebottle buzz from the smelly line of tide debris. Only one or two English visitors, or Sabbath-dressed natives, walked in the Sunday desertion.

At three in the afternoon Hugh's old green Triumph came over the hill. I got up and waved it down. Well, well, here we all are. Hugh and John both appeared to be in good order and much the same as usual, not that there was any reason why they should be different. The place and circumstances made it seem rather odd. They wanted something to eat. I reported that the Rum prospects were not all they might be but that we should be able to get a boat on Monday. Had Hugh got the rifle? Yes, all present and correct, and soft-nosed ammunition. Hugh had been on the road since Friday evening when he had left the office; he had slept in the car in the Welsh mountains for an hour or two

34

during the night. He had reached Anglesey early on Saturday, most of which he had spent waiting for John to lose a dinghy sailing race, Hugh chafing. They had had two or three hours sleep on a haystack on Saturday night, and since then had been driving steadily.

They at once changed into shorts, saying that this was a holiday. We bathed from a rock out in the bay and dried in the sun. I led the way back for tea at the Marine, two cars in close formation over the switchback road. Already we had got through a deal of Rum discussion, but it was a forbidden subject for hotel talk. Any thought of responsibility or conscience dropped with the arrival of the others, as I had hoped, and it did not rise again. It was absurd that I should ever have felt qualms. It was ridiculous that with three of us each forcing his ideas, his plans, his wishes, I had once, and gratuitously, been concerned about responsibility. Damn all that. Now that we were all present and in full voice, practical considerations were all that mattered. It was as much of an adventure as the impractical winter muse had naturally pictured it.

Hugh had hired the rifle in London. The permit was all in order and no questions had been asked. In the evening we went out to find a place where we might let off a few trial shots. There is a turning a few miles inland along the Mallaig road which goes off to the left and leads up the Morar River and along the shore of Loch Morar. The sun was low and yellow by now, midges in thick dances in the still air. We passed a few farms where uncut oats, or hay cocked up into domes in the northern fashion, led down to the loch shore. There was an ordinary telephone booth at the track-side, miles from anywhere. An Austin Seven stood beside a tent pitched on a perfect camp site of short flat turf, which was surrounded by birches except at its frontage of loch shore.

After this the road was soon impossible. We barged the car (Hugh's) through a bed of bracken but were halted by the disintegration of the track into a gully of loose rocks, which led on up and on round a headland. Here all the trackless mountains rose up from the loch and the path we were on petered out in a few yards. There was no sign of the works of crofters or shepherds or of any other man, only stones and heather. The evening light modelled the hills and the loch water was flat in evening calm.

The rifle was a beautiful little thing, a .256 Männlicher Carbine. It was short and squat, so that there was no need for it to be taken down and the fore-end extended to the muzzle. The arrangement of triggers was unfamiliar; of the two the second was a cocking trigger only and the front one let the thing off in the orthodox way. We went a little way round the headland and spread out a couple of hand-kerchiefs in the heather. Hugh lay down to take the first shot. The noise, absolutely catastrophic and unexpected, was so awful that we could only sit down and laugh. It was like thunder; like blasting. The trigger first released a deafening explosion which the hills took up and bandied to and fro, then thunder claps rolled around. The intervals were so long that it seemed a long wait between echo and re-echo, from cliff-face across miles of still air, again and again, gradually farther off and gradually dying. The slow, rolling majesty of the noise was incredible, so ponderous and lasting. Now where was our ignorant idea of a quick rifle report, a whiplash crack so short and sudden and lost in the hills that it would go unnoticed? For an illicit rifle report on Rum had rather worried us. The actuality was plain ridiculous, we could only listen to it, <u>listen</u> to it, and then laugh. There was nothing to be done about it, though the shattering of Sunday calm must gather every soul between Fort William and Mallaig.

I took a shot. The trigger was appallingly light and the recoil was heftier kick than a 12-bore's. You could not gently squeeze it; a barely appreciable touch sent it off and loosed the thunder, and once the long whine of a ricochet. The rifle was provided with a detachable telescopic sight which we fitted and tried. It was a nice thing to use and gave a good clear image. There was no adjustment for long range so we had to assume the trajectory was flat. You have to be careful with these things, to snuggle the rifle butt closely into the shoulder or the recoil might jerk the butt out of place and put the telescopic eyepiece into your eye. The handkerchiefs had three holes in them from four shots, so if we got within reasonable range of a stag and remembered the hair-light trigger, we had no excuse for missing.

The chugging of a motor boat sounded. It was coming across the loch towards us. We plumped down in the heather and lay still as the chugging came nearer. The midges were agony in our immobility. Probably the two men in the boat could not see us, but we could see them looking up at the slope where we lay. The boat chugged slowly, slowly, along the shore, close in. Then to our very great relief it turned away and went off across the water. We let it go to a safe distance and then went back to the car, which we urged from its bracken bed. The rifle was now rolled up and hidden within the tent – a safe way of carrying it about in public.

Trout were rising everywhere in the loch and the expanding ripples were long persistent on the absolute stillness of the surface. The loose sleepers of the bridge rattled under the car. We were high up, inland, and looking due west. The last of the light was behind the mountains of Rum, whose peaks were sharp monochrome shapes, as if cut out of cardboard. Behind us all the nearby hills were purple and red. The midges were so bad you could not even keep still to light a defensive pipe. When we came to the sea it was rippled and dark, a dim flat plain extending and darkening the silhouette of Rum.

John was saying that he would have come for this alone – it was new country to both him and Hugh. The arrangements had been left too vague for John and it was only the wish not to let down the expedition which had brought him north. I had overdone my pessimistic propaganda, thinking to forestall the disappointments I prophesied. He was all for organization; the boat should have been ready and waiting. I self-righteously considered I had done what I could in a short time, but in the process had untidily left too many clues in Mallaig. I still thought how odd that the enterprise had got even so far.

We went up to my attic in the Marine hotel. The proprietress had gaped visibly when I said we would all three share it. John spread out on the floor the two relevant sheets of the One Inch Ordnance Survey: the CUILLINS, RHUM & CANNA, Sheet 34 and SOUND of SLEAT, Sheet 35. There was not much room within the narrow varnished walls; the bed, wash-stand and chest of drawers took most of the floor space. I produced a bottle of whisky previously hidden in a drawer and we got down to the job.

The layout of this part of the West Coast and of its offlying islands is as follows: Rum and Eigg, as they say, Canna make Muck. These are the Small Isles; the Parish of the Small Isles. Muck is the smallest and most southerly; north-east and north of her lie Eigg and Rum. Rum is the largest, being eight miles by six; Canna lies north-west from Rum and their nearest points are only two or three miles apart across the Sound of Canna. The Small Isles group extends between about twelve and thirty miles south-west and west from Mallaig. Skye fills the northern horizon. Skye itself is separated from the Mainland by the narrow Sound of Sleat. Far outside Skye and the Small Isles is the long line of the Outer Isles; from the Butt of Lewis in the north to Barra Head in the south. The opposite sector of Mainland runs nearly north and south, is highly mountainous and is much indented with sea lochs.

Clear of Mallaig we should be sailing due west. The nearest point of Rum would be twenty miles away. When we got there we might have a look at the ground and then go elsewhere for the night. We might put in at Soay, a low island outlying from the south of Skye, or we might go further west and north to Canna, whose approach and harbour I knew from a visit two years before. Slack water tomorrow would be at dusk, or the ebb would then just be beginning. We could ground the boat at the top of the tide and get her off again at next high water. It was doubtful whether we could get a boat light enough to pull up easily, considering that only inboards were available. The weather was still the limiting factor. I was sure the break-up was on its way. It would be better to get to Rum in a heavy seaworthy boat, and have beaching troubles, than to be either prevented from starting or marooned by some cockle-shell.

We might even spend the night on Rum if prospects seemed good and unmolested. Getting on and off land would be the trouble. Anchoring off was unpractical. The boat would either have to be kept bumping in the surf, under supervision, which meant watches all night, or grounded at high water; or, if we landed at any other state of the tide, somehow dragged to high water mark. Then suppose that at the top of the tide we had got our heavy boat high and dry, and at low water we wanted to make a quick getaway? You couldn't very well hide a thing like a boat. If Rum officialdom became suspicious, as from an unaccountable rifle report for instance, the boat would soon be discovered.

Then the most tortuous degree of circumvolution in our return would avail us nothing. What did add to the difficulty was the very limited choice of landing places. There is no shelter all along the length of Rum's western coast. The south-westerly swell running unbroken from America would prevent a landing anywhere, even on a calm day. Most of the sheltered east coast was banned as being too near Loch Scresort, at whose head stands Kinloch Castle and attendant steadings. Loch Scresort in fact is the one and only anchorage where you could reasonably leave a boat to look after itself. That left the north and south extremities. The West Coast Pilot was briefly pessimistic. The only northern shelter is Kilmory Bay; 'not recommended as an anchorage'. It was very difficult.

We looked at the map of Rum, trying to visualise the lie of the land, to pick out corries by the contours, hidden ground, range of view of the castle and tracks to and from it. From the castle a dotted track led inland, due west, and then forked; one branch went north to meet the coast at Kilmory. The other branch turned south to reach the coast at a place marked by three dots and called Harris, with a fourth dot labelled 'Mausoleum'. One or two dots and 'Old Burial Ground' were marked at Kilmory. Knowing that Rum had once been crofted we considered houses, the dots on the map, to be safely ruined; except for the castle's satellites of course.

All plans were provisional until we could see the coast from a boat, close-to. You could hardly plan a stalk from a map of unknown country, without even knowing where the deer, if any, would be likely to be. But we reckoned, counting on a westerly wind, to get inland to such a position as would place us for a westerly stalk over high ground, and would lead us to the coast again.

John was concerned with tides and tide-streams and winds; he followed the West Coast Pilot keenly on these points. I, with less knowledge, assumed that the purpose of an engine was to deal with contrary wind or tide, and as for tide races, they would only race off headlands which could be seen, so why worry. One plan we did decide on. If we left Rum under suspicious circumstances we would land at a point of Mainland south of Mallaig, where there are plenty of little sandy inlets between the rocks. There we could dispose of any incriminating evidence, and return innocently to Mallaig, thus defeating a possible telephone message of appraisal to the Mallaig authority, the policeman himself.

There was a lot of argument about overnight accommodation in the Mallaig attic. Hugh determined to settle on the floor, a position for which he was increasingly envied as, on the bed, the struggles for the blanket intensified and the exchanges of knees became sharper. It was then very late.

Chapter Five

Monday

The young man whom Mr MacY had taken me to see on
Saturday evening was on the quay on Monday morning.
This was the man said to have cornered Mallaig lobster
distribution. I don't think he fished himself, but as a
middleman he parted the older men from their lobsters. He
was now talking business with a dour lobsterman from the
Isles, whom later we saw plod out for Canna in his heavy
west coast boat, the single cylinder Kelvin slowly plug-
plugging. The lobstermen come from outlying fishing-
crofting communities up and down the coast, or from the
Small Isles; they are slow and Gaelic-speaking. You could
not call parasitic the middleman who relieves them of the
responsibilities of rail and of dealing with the English.
Manchester was a good market for lobsters, said the
middleman. He certainly had made good; years ago, or in
remoter districts now, his affluence would have showed in
tweed and in heavy brogues from Inverness, but now in
Mallaig it was square-padded Burton shoulders, and hair
cream, and acuminate shoes; he had a pair in black suede
at home, very likely.

We never heard his name, but it was probably MacZ. Like so many of his countrymen he was kind and helpful without ever a thought of advantage. So, after he had rowed us to see his own boat, which was totally unsuitable, he ferried us about the harbour looking at other people's boats, in search of one which would do. His own boat was a long, narrow white motor launch, suitable for twenty people on a sight-seeing trip in calm water; chauffeur provided. The rowing boat he had borrowed to take us out in would have been more to the point. The next was a too-heavy motor boat, under-engined and high out of the water; no good.

After that there was a Swedish boat, about sixteen foot and partly decked, of odd but business-like lines, with sail and motor, jib and gaff-rigged mainsail and Austin Seven motor. It belonged to a young fisherman, MacZ said, who might be willing to hire. I thought the engine and gearbox had been lifted out of a car and adapted to run on paraffin, but Hugh said it was a proper marine unit, though neither of us knew much about it. The fourth and last boat was a light rowing boat with an engine of some sort and did not inspire confidence.

Now we turned back to the quay where the herring boats and the *Ossianic* were tied; at low water the most landward boats sit down on the sand, fended off from the quay and kept on even keel by fish boxes hung over the gunwale. They tie up there when something wants looking at below the water-line, or when the bottom is due for a scrub. Mr MacZ went off to look for the owner of the Swedish boat, which was the only possibility of the four available.

Scandinavian ships, small tough steamers or diesel boats, come every season to Scottish waters for the summer fishing. They anchor off the fishing centres, not to fish, but to buy mackerel from the herring drifters. The drifters get mackerel commonly enough, since their walls of net hanging in the sea cannot be choosing their fish. The home market for fresh mackerel is negligible and there is no market at all for cured mackerel, a processing to which this fish is not put in Britain. This is not so in Scandinavian countries. So their ships come to buy up British mackerel, to salt them down into barrels and take them home. The peculiar looking boat lying in Mallaig harbour was the common type of sixteen to eighteen footer carried by the mackerel steamers. I have heard that the Swedes like to sell off their boats in Scotland at the end of the season so as to procure both ready cash and to buy new boats next year.

The characteristic build of these boats gives them remarkable seaworthiness, but except in their degree of sheer, they don't look it. The stem is high, like a trawler's, but, to abandon seaside jargon, does not make an approximate right angle with the keel, as in the orthodox boat shape. Instead the stem slants steeply aft, and reaches down to the keel in a long slow curve; a curved stem with cut-away forefoot is something of the correct description, I believe. They have a heavy shouldered look; this is because of the exaggerated sheer and because the greatest beam is forward of amidships. But where the chief queerness of their looks lie is where my vocabulary fails. Perhaps a very marked reverse curve in the chine yet very shallow in the body? The result, anyway, is that their look is that of a floating dish, with very little freeboard amidships, and the planking slopes sharply in below the gunwale. They look as though nearly all of them is above the water, as a bird's curved breast feather floats on the surface.

We dangled our legs over the quay and looked at the Swedish boat, floating out on the still water. Mr MacZ was still looking for the owner. It was a sunny morning and hot; no trouble there, but the sky in the west did not look well. This particular boat (not that there can be more than very few British-owned Swedes) had been partly decked in by her owner. He had covered her in forward and carried the decking aft to make a surround, with combing, to the big cockpit. It was he, of course, who had put the Austin motor in her.

The owner, when he came, was another of the friendly ones. He was a young fisherman and going to sea the next day, but quite glad to hire. He would not be ashore again in time to receive his boat back into Mallaig. The boat, naturally, was the apple of his eye and he only hired her out when he wanted cash to carry out improvements; hence the motor and the decking of spruce. He rowed out to fetch her in from her moorings while we took our custom to Mr MacY, General Merchant. No business with stoves and pots and plates of course, simply bread and cheese and that sort of food, enough for a few days, and a can of fresh water. Also a bottle of whisky and some beer; it wasn't as if we had to carry it, and after all it was a gala occasion. The owner stocked up with fuel when we had settled the amounts; ten gallons of paraffin, four gallons of petrol, two quarts of engine oil. He took us on a demonstration run out of the harbour and showed us how to start the thing, keep it going and stop it. The engine drove the boat very briskly, but was fiendishly noisy and turned over at a great rate of revs. There was none of the slow chug of a fisherman's marine engine. It was the car-type transmission, gearbox, change lever and clutch, that made me think the engine had come out of a car. Besides, a seven horse-power marine unit would cost a hundred pounds.

At the quay the owner filled the fuel tanks, topped up the oil and handed over his boat. Spick and span, ropes neatly cheesed, bottom boards scrubbed clean; ready to steam all day, he said. Forward under cover where they would be dry, we stowed the tent wrapped round the rifle, the chocolate box of cartridges and the provisions. Then the fuel cans, the water and one rucksack each.

The engine started easily. We cast off, and moved out backwards in the whirring vibration of reverse common to all motorboats. We turned and left behind the casual watchers on the quay. The awful noise the motor made must be alright; the owner had not remarked on it but simply shouted above it. The noise was like a very old car engine running at full speed with no oil. Anyway we were really started; some small fruit at least for all the talk, talk, talk.

We cut inside the rock with its iron cage off the mouth of the harbour and headed out across the Sound for Point of Sleat. The ignition at retard soon warmed up the engine until it would accept paraffin. You could also half-close the cock on the water-pump inlet to heat it up quickly, but we did not care to meddle with this for fear of drying the engine.

Some sorts of pleasure craft were out in the Sound, though they were all heading south, down the mainland coast. Nothing accompanied us striking out to the west and by the time we had passed the Point of Sleat we had the sea to ourselves.

Inside the point was a little bay with crofts at its head; possible shelter there, or refuge, if called for. John concerned himself with the West Coast Pilot, but Kilmory in the north of Rum still seemed the only landing possibility, so we had better go and look at it and its prospects first.

We gave the Point a wide berth. The outlying rocks were collared with surf and dotted with cormorants; heavy-bodied black seafowl. They posed, sinister and heraldic, as they always appear when squatted in silhouette on some sea-washed rock. When they beat urgently, low over the waves, they are primeval flying machines, near-reptilian. John hadn't seen black guillemots before, which now sat about on the water; vermillion bills and plump black and white bodies. Or they flew, flickering black and white, demonstrating that their trailing legs and webbed feet were vermillion too. They are one of the nicest of all sea-birds, the neat sea pigeons. The puffins and razorbills floating on the water dived at the nearby noise of the engine. They had their callow young with them. It was already the beginning of the Scottish autumn.

We cleared Point of Sleat, then stopped the engine and lurched sluggishly in the swell. The sun had gone in, the sky had become overcast and now a steady drizzle began. Hugh, who would say, "let's bathe" if you took him to the seaside at Christmas, swam alongside. We had something to eat and drink, then shot at the bobbing empty bottles with my .22 pistol. At this point Eigg lay down in the south and Rum was up ahead, five or six miles away, filling the forward horizon. The high tops were masked in cloud. In the north the coast of Skye disappeared beyond the Point of Sleat, itself surrounded by Lochs Eishort, Slapin and Scavaig, and the lower parts of the Cuillin Hills made horizon fifteen miles away.

We finished eating and tried to sail without the motor, but the wind was too light; I doubt if we made one knot. We soon stowed the sails and got motoring again. The weather ahead and in the south-west looked worse. A great grey pall came up and the rain was soon heavy and steady. The light wind shifted about and the puffs freshened. The pall and the indecisive wind were held out by John as infallible signs of worsening weather. After all, the fine spell had looked like breaking up for days past.

We struck the coast of Rum at Loch Scresort, which nicely fixed our position and turned north across the mouth of the loch. This was by no means putting our heads in the lion's mouth because the loch runs nearly two miles deep inland. The castle appeared, red and modern-looking at the head of the loch; its tower showed but as the rain made for poor visibility we could not make out much and were content to go no closer.

Loch Scresort closed up astern and we steamed northwards, keeping about half a mile offshore, so as to have a good look at the coast. It was low, rocky and very inhospitable in the grey rain. There were short cliffs where the land met the sea and bare, broken rocks tumbled into the water. In places there were shingle beaches – until you were near enough to see the shingle become large boulders. A skin of sour turf grew between rocky outcrops of land and here and there were some patches of stunted birch. The picture was one of rainy desolation.

Suddenly there was a bunch of deer, close to the coast. Excitement ran so high that at once we turned to charge the land. Increasing engine noise soon moved the deer. They set off inland at a brisk trot, halting to look back; their spread ears looking very large. They were soon out of sight. The immediate impulse was to dash after them, but this was no way to go at the matter. In any case we soon realised that the group had been hinds, which were perfectly inadequate; obviously we had to qualify with a proper stag, or not at all. Besides, it was rather close to the castle. However there was a tiny bay nearby so we turned into it, shut off the motor and poled in with the oars until the keel grounded. Hugh jumped out into the water; first landing on Rum. We took a photograph of his feet, under a foot of water, standing on the boulders of Rum. This place was a narrow strip of boulders laid in a cleft between the cliffs. The boulders were piled steeply and covered with a green algal slime. Sunlight would have made the water sparkle where it lapped the stones; the rain made it desolate. As a landing place, it was hopeless on all counts. Hugh hoisted his wet trousers up the mast and we set off along the coast.

Those first deer were a happy sight. They seemed unlikely to me; an improbable fauna. They were too large to be real untamed, British wild animals. The sodden and barren coast should have supported a few posturing cormorants on the rocks (they were there alright), some noisy oystercatchers along the tide line, stray meadow pipits in the wet grass – not these animals like slim-legged calves. The first sight of a seal's head rising from the sea – a big dog's head suddenly seen in the midst of the waters – has the same surprising unlikeliness. Not that one's imagination, confined to Britain of course, could supply an environment for either red deer or grey seal which would remove the oddness of that first meeting. Still, there the deer had been, large and wild, and apparently quite at home. Well, well. For practical; that is, destructive purposes it was encouraging to know that there were at least some deer on Rum, and reasonably approachable by the look of it.

From Loch Scresort round to Kilmory Bay by sea is six or seven miles. We followed the trend of the coast to the north and then to the north-west and Eigg closed up behind the near horizon of Rum. Once Eigg had gone, we rounded the most northerly point of Rum to open Canna. The coastwise course was westerly now, with Rum on the left, Canna some six miles ahead and to the right, Skye filling the northern horizon. The island of Soay, thought of as a possible refuge to run for from Rum, showed in the north as a low-lying dark hump. It sprawled across the sea between us and Skye.

Once round the north point we soon opened Kilmory Bay. It came into sight as a broad curve of sand, a crescent formed where a wide, flat-bottomed valley met the sea. Sand dunes and the broad floor of sand divided the sea from the grass. The valley gradually narrowed inland, until it was closed by great mountains. At once we saw the disturbing sight of two well-preserved houses – those that on the map we had dismissed as ruins. One was small with a corrugated iron roof while the other looked the ordinary modern type of crofter's house. Both were set down on the short seaside turf and were entirely without environs; no path or fence or garden and the turf growing up to the walls all round. The two houses were not all. The dotted track of the map translated into a road which ran due inland, accompanied by a row of telegraph poles. The coastal end of the wires was delivered into a wooden hut. The cable evidently went on from there, across the floor of the sea, probably to Skye. It was enough to put anyone off.

Nobody suggested turning in however. We continued on our way across the bay, intending to go exploring along the coast. But then we saw that the windows of the bigger house looked as if they were shuttered. We had a sudden access of boldness. The helm went hard over and we drove in towards the sandy crescent. Ho, we stood in for Kilmory Bay.

The keel ground gently on the sand. We looked closely for any sign of a human being but there was none. John and Hugh jumped out and splashed about through the small surf. I dropped anchor a little way out and waited for them. It was still raining hard. They walked off across the sand towards the houses. I saw them looking in at the windows. They came back to say that the houses were empty and locked but had been recently inhabited as there were books lying on the table. As this seemed reasonably safe we brought the anchor ashore and pushed off the boat. The offshore wind should keep her out against the flowing tide, but if it didn't the small surf would not matter. We went away to explore the Kilmory district.

The two houses and the telegraph hut were a little offset from the mouth of the valley. We turned to walk inland and were greeted by such a sight. The whole broad grassy floor of the valley was dotted with deer, quietly grazing. There were scores of them. The valley floor was flat, approximately a quarter of a mile across and stretching a mile deep into the land before the hills began to close in to constrict it. A stream with mallard dotted about it came meandering down the middle. The straight road was cut into the hillside of the valley's western bank.

The sight of the deer was like a shot from an African big game film; the screen filled with numberless grazing herds ranged across the wide country. I believe between two and three hundred deer were grazing the Kilmory river pastures in that moment. The nearest animals were very touchy and we were careful not to disturb them. Those that we could see were hinds or calves.

While we were wondering at the sight, Hugh made an exclamation and laughed. I thought he had seen something sufficiently catastrophic to be funny. It was a group of white ponies. This unsettling evidence of domesticity caused a flutter until we realised they were the deer ponies which had not yet been rounded up. We came across a rough shed open at the front and overgrown with nettles. There was straw on the mud floor and in the middle of it lay a dead deer. Dead of natural causes, we hoped. It was whole, but clearly long dead. Nearby were the traces of two stone crofts.

More nettles; Kilmory had evidently once been a little crofting community. I wondered if the crofters had abandoned it of their own accord, or more likely been cleared during the nineteenth century. Evictions were common then to make way for sheep walks: first landlord's notice, then the call of the emigration ship, then sheep. When sheep no longer paid, thousands of acres of sheep walk were turned over to deer forest. I don't know whether Rum ever had the intermediate period of sheep farming.

We found 'Old Burial Ground' of the map – a circular patch of tall seeded grass within a stone wall. Some rough stones rose out of the grass but we could not investigate them as they were in full sight of the valley-full of deer. We never had the chance to read the inscription on the one inscribed gravestone; the others might have been stone gateposts. Leaning against the graveyard wall, in the rain, we watched the grazing herds and the smaller groups and the scattered animals that were browsing singly.

The long line of sand dunes lay behind to seaward. In places there were miniature undercut cliffs of sand whose overhanging brinks were bearded with grass. The river trickled across the broad beach. It was of small shingle, the river water spreading over it two or three inches deep. The sweep of sand, its half mile crescent, was generally more than a hundred yards across and was broken by reefs. Offshore were surf-capped rocks with seaweed round them. The boat at the rim of the sea was a long way off; Hugh's forlorn trousers flapping at the mast head.

Already the short grass was soggy and the loose sand was firmed with rain. Lichened rocks above high water mark were slimy with the wet. Everywhere deer hoof prints marked the sand, which was also littered with their dung. They came down to browse seaweed, of course.

With the offshore wind in the south-west Kilmory Bay was quite nicely sheltered. But even while we explored the wind shifted into the west to blow along the shore and the surf increased. It was getting towards dusk. We were doubtful whether we could reach shelter anywhere other than Rum before darkness fell. We had seen nobody, the deer grazed undisturbed in their wonderful hundreds and it was a foul evening, so we thought it best to camp down for the night, there and then, on forbidden ground. The latest of all plans had not considered actually camping in a tent on Rum, but now circumstances, the weather particularly, called for it. The wind was quickly freshening and the rain never let up.

At high water the eastern end of Kilmory Bay is shut off by a reef which is thirty or forty yards short of the terminal rocks, and at these rocks the coast again turns into low cliffs. This reef thus closes off a little secondary bay, secluded against the shameless expanse of Kilmory main bay. The boat in this retreat would be a little less obvious to one and all, so we moved her along. A flat patch of turf immediately adjacent to the sand made a good tent site, and was backed inland by rocks. Thus tent and at any rate most of the boat would not be visible from the road or telegraph box.

I remember us getting the tent up – flapping wet canvas, flapping oilskins, sheeting rain, numbed hands. We brought everything ashore, wrapped it in groundsheets and put it under the lee of rocks near the tent. We all squeezed into the tent and changed into spare dry clothes. It was passably cosy and we managed to get warm, though the tent was a very old one of John's which leaked and was only built to accommodate two persons. But it was better indoors with groundsheets to cover the wet grass, and malignant nature shut outside.

I had noticed grass of Parnassus thereabouts. It grew in permanently wet places in the grass further back from the shore. It was confined to the narrow strip of seaside turf which had a depth of soil beneath it. Its range stopped with the beginning of the rough inland tussocks and rock and heather patches. The white buttercup flowers had a look of rareness, they opened singly on green stems upstanding from the squishy turf; a single heart-shaped leaf clasped each stem half way up its height. The Kilmory rocks, the thin strata eaten away at the edges, were exactly like piles of mouldering books on a larger scale, each leaf distinct. There was something after all in the mineral wealth of Rum; not, I'm afraid, our golden or Fuller's earthy treasures of the hinterland, but something. The West Coast Pilot said, 'A remarkable geological feature is the vein of bloodstone at the north-western end of the island, which, however, is not considered worth working.'

We lay in the tent, often opening the flap to look out at the boat bumping in the flooding tide, and at the driven smoke of rain. Rain pocked the surf as it swilled up the firm sand. We went out frequently to pull in the boat to keep her up with the tide. How perfectly were we involved in the break-up of the fine spell – it was timed to the very day. There was no call now to bother over the Rum authorities; whether they discovered us or not, we were weather-bound for the night. Our concern was what to do with the boat. The wind was still rising across the bay, where it kicked up a short sea.

High water came at dirty dusk. We gave the boat a final heave and brought the anchor inland. The boat now fixed us for the night, however we liked it; she would be high and dry until next high water. Tomorrow would be Tuesday, the day the owner might arrive at his island, *vide* Mr MacY of Mallaig. As I have said before however, our planning had never practically considered the island personnel, due to lack of knowledge. Official Tuesday movements were merely a chance to us, they might or might not be beneficial to the cause. Here we were on Rum, for better or for worse; we could not take into account the hypothetical movements of its staff.

We managed to all lie down endways in the tent, head to feet alternately. The rifle was no sort of bedfellow, being hard and knobbly and there was no dry space for it at either end, nor between us. It fitted partly into a limp canvas 12-bore case which Hugh had brought, and which was too long, so that the end flapped like a sock several sizes too big, whose extremity the toes cannot attain. We stood the rifle on its butt and tied it to the tentpole with a handkerchief.

Chapter Six

Tuesday

The prospect without was nasty. It was just light and cold and windy – the time of shivery dawn cold when you want only to snuggle back to the stored night warmth, and go on sleeping. We got out of the tent and into wet oilskins; chattering cold, dispersing the precious heat. Hugh and I were going off stalking straightaway, in this safest time of early morning. Then we saw we could not leave the boat as she was.

As she had settled, the tide leaving her, she had dug herself a grave in the sand. She was now embedded, solid as a rock, on an even keel. We tried all three together to jar her, to see how solidly she was in but she did not budge an inch. It was as if she was cemented in. One blade of the propeller was buried and the keel was between six inches and a foot deep in all along its length. The tide was hurrying up again, spring tides and on the make; she would only bury herself deeper.

We would have to dig her out, that was all, then somehow get her above high water mark. The prospect looked entirely hopeless, especially at that time of the morning, with wet, cold hands, bare feet in wet sand and cutting wind and we were altogether inclined towards a psychological low ebb.

We began to dig with oars and it was miserable until we were warm. We dug and scooped and dug until we had cleared one side down to the iron shod keel. Then we tilted the boat over and cleared the other side. She was so heavy that when she lay over on her side the three of us could only just heave her back to even keel. Now to get her out of the pit!

The rocks were well littered with pit-props and heavy driftwood. This was great luck as we could not possibly have done it otherwise. The next stage was to get rollers crosswise under the keel. We started at the stern, levering with pit-props. Sometimes the fulcrum was on a log on the nearside of the keel, as a see-saw and the lever was pressed down. Or the fulcrum was on the far side of the keel and the pole was strained upwards. The First and Second Orders of Levers? When the pole got a good bite it gave as much as a two inch lift to the keel – a profit hastily secured with stones and blocks jammed underneath. Very gradually we managed to work pit-props under the keel, though many of them snapped, being sea-rotted. The ends of the logs lay on the edge of the pit round the boat, which thus gradually gained clearance under the keel. Then we dug and worked the boat's thwarts lengthwise under the ends of the rollers, to make a railway for them, the boat meantime propped on an even keel. At that we were ready for the first heave. The tide swirled into the pit around the propeller. One, two, six, Hup! She moved an inch or two forward. But the worst was done, and we kept ahead of the tide. She went quite easily, considering her weight and the upwards gradient of the beach. We shoved in short stages of a few inches, keeping her upright and moving the boards and rollers, until she was safely above the high water mark, then we left her on rollers, in pit-prop stilts. It had taken three solid hours. That was the start of the day's work. If it had made one thing impossible, it was a quick getaway. It was unavoidable, although it increased the precariousness of our position here on Rum. Anything as tying as an immobile boat was unfortunate.

Now that the whole of the boat could be seen, her full shape showed that the waterline impression of a floating dish was perfectly misleading. For she had a quite deep, long keel which would prevent her crabbing sideways in a following sea, and which was deep enough to keep her from making much leeway when sailing near the wind. However this was no time to stand admiring the product of our labours.

Hugh and I prepared to go off stalking at once. Oilskins, rifle, cartridges, field glasses, whisky. Hugh slung the rifle, inside its canvas case, by a string over his shoulder, then put his oilskin on over the top. The rifle hung down at his side, so that he looked blameless, unless a slight stiffness in his walk was suspicious.

"For God's sake don't get caught", John said as we walked away. Famous last words? We went along the coast a little way to the east, away from the bay, then turned sharply inland, meaning to bear west and return to work the eastern ridge of the valley.

We had hardly turned inland when we sighted a stag. He was on the skyline ahead. We plumped down instantly and viewed his thin stilt-legs through a screen of out-of-focus grasses. He went down into dead ground almost at once. We thought to come up with him again by making a wide detour and approaching his estimated position upwind.

This strategy kept involving us with bunches of hinds. There were too many deer about, that was the trouble and the great majority were hinds and calves – hind-calves and

Robert Atkinson and John Ainslie on North Rona, 11 August 1936
© estate of Robert Atkinson

Hugh LeLacheur on the Fort William to Mallaig road, 'the worst 'A'
road in the British Isles ...' © estate of Robert Atkinson

The site of target
practice by Loch
Morar, which drew the
motor-boat from
Lettermorar on the
opposite shore
© estate of Robert
Atkinson

Robert's elegant (borrowed) roadster contrasts with Hugh's elderly
Triumph, both casually parked outside Mallaig post office © estate of
Robert Atkinson

Steam drifters in Mallaig harbour, with the railway pier behind
© estate of Robert Atkinson

Robert and John Naish wait to negotiate with the Swedish boat's
owner © estate of Robert Atkinson

Leaving Mallaig, John consulting the 'West Coast Pilot',
Robert at the tiller © estate of Robert Atkinson

Calm sea in Cuillin Sound, the hills of Rum clear ahead
© estate of Robert Atkinson

First brief landing on the east coast of Rum
© estate of Robert Atkinson

Ashore at Kilmory Bay
© estate of Robert
Atkinson

Kilmory, the second bay. Boat at the high water mark wedged with pit-props © estate of Robert Atkinson

At the tent site, Kilmory Bay. Compass Head, Canna, prominent on the horizon © estate of Robert Atkinson

Robert spying the ground for a stag
© estate of Robert Atkinson

Robert taking the shot
© estate of Robert Atkinson

The 'John MacNab' moment ... Robert posing with the stag,
16 August 1938 © estate of Robert Atkinson

John and Hugh with the boat ready to launch from Kilmory Bay
© estate of Robert Atkinson

Readying the boat to leave Canna
© estate of Robert Atkinson

Robert at the tiller sailing out from Canna
© estate of Robert Atkinson

Rum hills and a following sea in Cuillin Sound
© estate of Robert Atkinson

Robert (left) with John at the tiller, expecting the worst
© estate of Robert Atkinson

Threatening waves, Hugh with one hand on the pump
© estate of Robert Atkinson

The Swedish boat back in her berth, undamaged, except for
scraped paint © estate of Robert Atkinson

The stag on the wall, journey's end for a fine eight pointer, Henley on Thames, September 1938 © estate of Robert Atkinson

Robert at the wheel of the newly acquired 'Heather,' 13 August 1939 © estate of Robert Atkinson

knobbers, I suppose (see any natural history book). Each lot we came upon had to be carefully circumvented; often we could not help moving the deer. Halting often, we searched the changing view of country for men or for suspicious movements of deer. We saw nothing untoward, but often picked up previously unseen deer. We were on low ground all this time, though it was uneven enough to afford cover. There were rock ridges, rough grassy slopes and boggy dells. Herbage grass and heather only grew on the higher places or on well-drained slopes. We happened often upon deer 'forms' – flattened patches in the grass where the deer had been lying. Deer slot and dung were everywhere.

We crawled about unsatisfactorily for a long time, continually put off our original detour by hinds, which were very touchy. Meanwhile the stag became lost, until what was probably he was finally seen taking to the hills, with many backward glances. We also sighted and made short excursions after other stags. We became very hot and suffered several alarms. One particular whistle was horribly unsettling as it was so very human, but there was nothing to be seen and we could only carry on, though feeling disturbed. About the same time a very doggy bark was heard, which also caused anxiety. We did not know that hinds barked until afterwards, when it was no comfort. The stalking would have been pleasurable in an unhurried peace of mind but nervous alertness rather spoilt it. A cat cannot feel comfortable on hot bricks. Up to leaving the tent we had done nothing irremediable, so we could probably have faced the authorities and got away with it, if we had kept the rifle hidden. Now of course things were different.

We drank from the streams we crawled through, or up, or down. After several hours we had spoilt the ground, sent several bunches of hinds and two or three stags off to the hills, and had only one or two might-have-beens for reward.

We felt we surely ought to be able to get a shot at a stag – we had seen several and they were reasonably approachable. Damn all those blasted hinds. So far we had nibbled at a large patch of ground only to spoil it. We had better go and crawl elsewhere.

There were ravens and hooded crows about, blown out of stately flight by the wind, which carried their croaks. We noticed these things quite ordinarily, except for rather a lack of interest. We put up a covey of grouse which whirred away clucking, "go-beck, go-beck"-ing so loudly that you wanted to whisper fiercely, "Hush!" The wind was blustery and strong all the morning and quick rain squalls alternated with diluted sunshine. We moved westwards until we came to a place which commanded a view of all the valley and its opposite bank and over there were several stags, standing about in green bracken. They were about a mile away. The floor of the valley was still covered with deer, the grazing herds dotted all the green grass by the winding river. We saw a flight of wild duck plane down to the water. The white ponies were still there. It would have been a parkland scene if the country had been compressed and given trees. In patches of sunlight, stags' antlers were perfectly white; they were in velvet at this season. The nap looks white in sunshine, like lichen on a west coast tree or on an old crooked billet of blackthorn. The top branches of a dead tree, whose finer frith has been taken by the winds, looks chalk-white sometimes – as when seen from sunward, in level winter sunshine and the stags' antlers looked like that, branch and colour of an old bough.

We chose and marked as best we could a group of half a dozen stags resting in the bracken of the opposite hillside. The hillside above the road grew bracken patches and it looked steep and rocky. We marked down a broken wall running down the hillside near the stags and to the seaward side of them; we hoped to be able to pick up and recognise this wall when we came stalking from seaward. If the stags stayed put we should probably not see them until we were pretty close and the wall would be a warning.

We began the long approach to those stags with the best part of two miles to cover. The open country was painful; somehow one's imagination, set to stalking, had always claimed such cover as birch woods, deep stream gullies, boulder-strewn slopes, as given. It had never accounted for this, which was, in fact, open moorland. One's rear felt undefended. We walked back to the shore, keeping out of sight of the valley, whose mouth we crossed by the sand dunes. The sand was criss-crossed with our footmarks of yesterday, more unfortunately tell-tale than anything else. We paddled through the river where it issued across the shingle, walked inland past the telegraph box, the shed with the dead deer and the remains of the two crofts to 'Old Burial Ground'. The real stalk began from there.

Cover was good for two hundred yards. It led us a long crawl through soaking bracken, along ditches, through little bogs and under broken-down stone walls. That accomplished, we had to make height, so we left the good cover of the valley edge to stalk a slanting line up the hillside towards the old wall – the one we had marked from the other side of the valley about an hour before. The wall was hidden by the slope of the hill, but if we kept to a line going upward and inland we must strike it.

This line often exposed us, of necessity, to the full view of the valley hinds. Our first care was to keep them quiet. Later on they would be bound to get our wind, but we should be further away from them then. As it was, one or two of them occasionally turned to face us, broad ears stuck out sideways. They looked very leggy. Our progress was extremely tedious, *ventre à terre* all the way now, when before we had crawled. We came unexpectedly on to the road. I felt foolish squirming across it. It was a good flint road and only overgrown with grass in the middle. Always we kept stopping to see to the valley deer, to scan all the distant ground for men or unaccountable movements of deer or for birds disturbed into the air; but the view was always serene.

Once above the road the ground was more broken, with rock outcrops and bracken and deep heather. We were in sight of the valley floor only occasionally and then for short spaces between covering rocks. The hinds gradually grazed their way up the valley. Some of them were a little upset, but the general movement was as of cattle grazing across a meadow, moving a few paces and stopping to graze, and moving again. Some were lying down and only moved as they got left in the rear. It was a good thing to have them a little further removed from our operations and they would still present a picture of grazing calm to any possible observer who might take a distant look over the valley.

We stopped now and then to rest. The whisky bottle had a quotation printed on it, I can now only remember the first line:

Land of the mountain and the flood
Something something shaggy wud

Or alternatively,

Land of the mountain and the flude
Something something shaggy wood.

It became a sort of trade-mark, or password, often recited during the rest of the trip. We had had no food all day, we were very wet and hot and had sore knees. All that work with the boat and then the stalking was enervating. It was correct to carry a dram with you and so, presumably, to use it, unsuitable as it was to the physical mood.

We found the broken down wall and kept on and up. The stags were still there. Fearful excitement! There were a least a dozen scattered about the hillside, in twos or threes and some of them were lying down in the bracken. They were above us on the hillside, a long way further on. The stalk was very slow and laborious and we found that we rested when we could. As we got nearer the stags appeared uncomfortable. We took a longer rest against a rock.

Most of the stags' coats were pale against the bracken and grass but one or two of them appeared darker, almost chestnut. The white antlers looked quite close now. But they were disturbed, and – oh hell! – they began to move off. They were to windward of us, but afterwards we discovered a reverse wind current which carried uphill at ground level, against the prevailing westerly blow and I suppose below it; in any case directly from us to the stags.

However, of the dozen-odd stags we had seen, five stayed behind. We wormed closer, meticulously careful and they had not moved when we reached the haven of a big rock and could sit upright. We sat in a little world bounded by sky. The valley floor was well out of sight and the stags were behind the rock, up the hillside. You had only to peep round to see them. They were not more than a hundred yards away. Hugh unslung the rifle. The moment had come, if the stags would just stay still for two minutes. They hadn't looked like moving. We tossed for the shot and it fell to Hugh. He began to pull the rifle out of its case. I peered round the rock, my face in the grass, to see the stags move off unhurriedly and disappear over the skyline.

We went heedlessly to the top of the ridge, only being careful to give a searching look over new ground as it opened, in case of a stray stag, but we did not see the five again. At the top we put up a covey of grouse which went off with their usual appalling noise. We had been speaking in whispers all day. A flat patch at the edge of the hill had a small, neatly built cairn in the middle of it. There was a pole trap on top of it. It is illegal to set these traps in the open, I believe. The trap was rusty but set. Any evidence of man was disquieting – not that we had been in anything but a state of extreme nervous tension all day – but the trap was disturbing in that context. Without it there would have been nothing to show that anyone had ever trodden that ground before. As it was it showed that the ground was regularly patrolled. I wondered incidentally if the trap had anything to do with the complaints of those Skye shepherds about the golden eagles of Rum. I was sorry not to see any eagles. The trap could only have been set for eagles or buzzards as it was cunningly placed, commanding miles of country to the east; just the place a bird of prey would choose for a sitting out post.

A little way further on there was another trap similarly laid out and set. When I squirmed to the edge of the little grassy plateau on which the cairn was built, I looked down onto two stags. I didn't expect them to stay for a shot as they were upset and on the move. By the time the rifle was ready they had crossed the road below and were too far away.

We should soon have to give up and return to John, if we were to get away from Rum and reach alternative shelter by daylight. We were tired and discouraged and we had been crawling fruitlessly about for about seven hours. We decided that we must move to fresh ground again, this time for a last try. Kilmory was extremely difficult country, but, knowing nothing of the distribution of the deer, when we saw a stag we naturally went after it. We did not go first to easy stalking ground and then look for stags.

Now we turned west, away from Kilmory and all its works, and walked straight into the wind. Two miles on that line would lead to the next 'village', marked on the map as two houses and named Guirdil, on the north-west coast. We had rather given up hope, because there were no sign of any deer ahead and we had spoilt the ground behind.

We went on, up and down some parallel valleys, crossing the stream at the bottom of each. Then we saw two stags, browsing just below the skyline. They were rather a long way ahead but dead to windward. It was easy ground. We hardly had to do more than stoop to keep out of sight and often could walk upright. We were soon quite close. The last twenty-five yards were a crawl, leading to a grassy crest. I squirmed up and looked through the grasses to the other side. There were two stags on the next crest and clear air between us – they were against the sky, side by side on the horizon, about a hundred and fifty yards away. I wriggled back. Quick fumbling to get the rifle out, the telescopic sight on, then the thumb screws that held it tightened. Now – cartridges. We had a quick fierce argument in whispers, debating who was to shoot. Hugh had carted the rifle all the time, we'd tossed up before and it had fallen to him. This was no time for arguing. Hugh was determined to be unselfish: "It was your idea, I wouldn't think of taking the shot." I didn't care who shot as long as somebody did. Hugh slipped a cartridge into the breech, pushing the breech-bolt forward and over. I took the rifle and wriggled back to the crest.

With both elbows firm in the grass, the butt settled comfortably into my shoulder. The stag was clear in the field of the telescopic sight, but not large. I was perfectly steady and was surprised at it even in that moment. But I felt the awful momentousness of the occasion. I cocked the striker with the back trigger and moved my forefinger to

65

the front trigger. The one and only chance. Hold your breath, gun squeezed tight, last steadying in the sights – the lightest touch on the front trigger.

It went off; the explosion, the bucking recoil. The stag did not waver, he pitched forward instantly and lay on his back. I watched this happen without elation. I felt unmoved – the reaction, as after a near-accident in a motor car, was delayed. The second stag hesitated a moment, then made off. The report had not echoed, for all the Mainland example and the explosion died away on the wind. I turned to tell Hugh that it was alright.

It was a rotten shot though and the stag was not killed. Through field glasses I saw that he was hit through the spine. He began to struggle downhill towards us, dragging paralysed hindquarters. Hugh quickly shoved in another cartridge, waited his moment, and fired. The stag lay over and did not move again. I could see the two bullet holes through the glasses. Hugh's was plumb central and it must have gone straight through the heart.

Well, it was done. We put the rifle back in its bag and picked up the empty cartridge cases. The shot had gone across the top of the narrow valley; as we hurried down into it towards the stag we came to the stream at the bottom. This stream, running quietly in the grass, suddenly dropped a sheer twenty feet into the earth although the ground level had not changed. The stream went over the drop in a thin waterfall, to a tiny pool with bare ground around it at the bottom. The brink was overhung and overgrown. It would be just the place to tip the corpse.

I remember exactly the sight of the stag lying on its side in the grass, even as I can still conjure up in my mind a picture of it as seen through the telescopic sight (centred to the black dot). It lay on its left side. The second bullet hole was bubbling scarlet with arterial blood, and already it buzzed about with flies. Both bullets had come out on the other side. We looked at the coarse hair of the beast's coat, and the unfamiliar branch of antlers. Where was the Monarch of the Glen in the Landseer tradition? The corpse was that of an inoffensive-looking herbivore, with large bovine eyes, gentle and unintelligent. I would avoid the hypocrisy of saying the death caused regret; one felt a sort of worry at having destroyed anything so large. It took us both to drag it, we grasped a pair of legs each and hauled it to the edge of the ravine. Its mouth fell open, its teeth clanked, and its tongue hung out.

We were now in a state; very nervous and wanting to hurry away from the place. As in children's ghostly games, the perpetrators get the worst fright. We cut off the creature's head with Hugh's penknife. This was not as difficult as it sounds, but took several minutes. We whispered still and continually glanced to the skyline; the horror of somebody appearing over it was not to be thought of – but we must have half-expected it since we looked up so frequently. The mess of blood from the carotid artery and the great veins made decapitation difficult. We managed to find the atlas vertebra and worked the head to and fro, I cutting at the tendons, until the head came away in Hugh's hands. We then cut off other parts which it is correct to take from a stag.

"Is that all you want?" We heaved the corpse over the brink and it crashed into the pool with an almighty splash. It looked very natural, a plausible accident even, except that it had no head. It was only visible from above. We rinsed the blood off our hands in the stream, picked up the rifle and the severed head and hurried from the scene.

The walk back to the camp was most uncomfortable, with the incriminating and bloody head plain for all to see. We came out by the houses, having hurried in stops and starts, one of us often going forward to reconnoitre. The head was surprisingly heavy and we carried it by the antlers between us. Its mouth dropped open, and, the tendons being cut, the tongue hung out its full length and the teeth continually clanked. We had to cross the wide stretch of Kilmory Bay. Although we kept to the sand dunes as best we could, we were often visible for miles, giving a feeling of nakedness; even as one might feel bathing naked on a wide open beach and liable to sudden interruption. When we came near the tent I went forward alone, just in case. All was well. John was inside the tent. He had not heard the shot; neither had he sight nor sound of anyone during all the long day. He would not believe that we had killed a stag. I waved Hugh to come on, but, not understanding and playing safe, he came empty-handed. John would not believe the stag until we had fetched it. Then he was quite overcome, freely admitting that success was the last thing he had expected of our stalk. We quickly stowed the head and the rifle well out of sight in the bows of the boat. It was not a fine head but it had antlers, so it qualified as a stag and that was all we had come for.

Now to get away, as quickly as might be. But first Hugh and I had to have a bite of food, the first of the day. We all squeezed into the tent, pleased and excited, and ate and talked and finished off the last of the beer. John's long day must have been very trying, wondering what was going on and with nothing to do. We had been away about ten hours. It was now about six o'clock in the evening.

The tide was low but flowing again. We had a long way to move the boat. We struck the tent, cleared the site and loaded everything into the boat. Getting the boat down to the sea was two hours of uneventful labour; turning her round to face the sea and holding her upright were the worst parts. We moved her a foot at a heave, taking up the railway behind and laying it ahead. She kept coming off the rollers. It was an unkind repetition of our dawn labour. Holding up the boat gave me a raw bruise on the hip, which stuck to my shirt for days afterwards. The sea had looked nasty all day but had perhaps gone down a little now. As we worked, the *Lochmor* passed, pitching steeply, on her way to Canna. She had come from Mallaig via Loch Scresort, where, perhaps, she had dropped the proprietor. That didn't matter now. We cleared the camp-site so that there was no sign of occupation, except for the flattened patch where the tent had stood; already the pressed grasses were springing back. Otherwise the only evidence we left was the thoughtless footprints all over Kilmory sands, and, of course, the corpse in the waterway.

We propped the boat in the surf and waited for the tide to float her. We had rolled her about twenty five yards. There was a rather nasty surf. We threw away the props as they floated off, then, when she began to bump, half-buoyant, took off our trousers and worked her out through the breakers. Hugh got in, ready to row, I meanwhile trying to keep her head-on. Hugh said afterwards that it was a desperately hard pull against wind and tide. It looked anxious to me at the tiller, trying to clear the reef which cut off our landing place from the rest of Kilmory Bay. The wind made its fierce whine in the rigging. It was difficult trying to locate off-lying rocks under the choppy water although some seaweed did show as darker patches. John and Hugh managed it and we made the open water of the bay. I went to the engine and wound the flimsy erection of handle, bicycle chain and freewheel; you had delicately to pick off the chain once the engine was running. We were surprised when it fired at first swing, and, after a little further cranking, ran. It ran on three cylinders for a time, then as it dried out and warmed, the fourth came in and all fired evenly. We shipped oars, put on trousers again, and turned out away from Rum. It was a relief finally to be clear of the place. I admit though that our failure even to sight a man on Rum rather spoils the story. A judicious use of fiction could have prevented this tameness.

We chose to aim for Canna, five or six miles to the west with a head-sea all the way. The engine clattered away inside its matchboarding box; you might not sit on or touch the box because the revs screamed if you did. This was because the throttle control came out through the after end of the box, which was loose and when the box moved the throttle moved with it.

There was a big swell outside the bay, but it was a joy to feel the boat drive at it. She never attempted to dig her bows into the seas, but rather pounded them, chucking spray up in clouds. Her bows were of the build which invariably drenches her passengers. The skyline was the running top of the swell. The wind picked up the spray and flung it yards, a stinging sheet. The boat handled beautifully, barging and bumping and pitching, yet driving ahead at a good speed. The short passage to Canna was exhilarating. The salt caked on our eyelashes.

Canna harbour is the water enclosed by Canna herself and its subsidiary, Sanday. It is roughly oblong, open only to the east. We passed the steamer pier on Canna but rejected it as too exposed; a boat moored there would bump badly. We went further in and tied up at the stone jetty in front of the laird's house. The laird came out to ask our intentions and we asked permission to camp for the night. He at once offered the barn, and said that we should get milk and eggs at the farmhouse. His car was outside the house so he made us put our gear into the car, to be driven to the barn. We left rifle and stag's head hidden in the bows of the boat. I knew this barn of old. When I had been to Canna before, to look for nesting shearwaters, we (there were two of us then) had been put up in the barn, through the good offices of the proprietor of that time. The present laird was new; Canna had changed hands, lock stock and barrel, the year before. The new laird had imported the first motor car to be landed on Canna. It is a nice island, one which has a kindly, fertile and prosperous look. There are about fifty inhabitants – fishermen and farmers (one of the nicest fishermen is called McIsaacs). There is a school, a shop which is the wooden hut by the pier, a post office and two churches, one Protestant and one Roman Catholic. Everyone you meet is kindly. Larch and sycamore grow there, almost enough to make woods; a rich change from Rum's barrenness. There is a mile or two of rough track for the pioneer motor car to run along.

The then laird was a young man. He was taking the car along to a place near the barn, to try gassing rabbits with the car's exhaust, so he took our gear along with him. The barn is a large building, stone-built and buttressed, well away from other buildings. The loft at one end has a fireplace and is reached by an outside stone staircase; the upstairs was our quarters. There were some lumps of coal outside and plenty of wood so we got a tremendous fire going. There was straw for beds.

From our doorway we watched the laird and a friend gassing rabbit burrows. They did not succeed in bolting any rabbits; the noise of the engine probably kept them underground. After dusk we returned to the boat and brought the rifle to the loft, to be cleaned and oiled and for its case to be dried. Then, being finished with it, it was once more wrapped within the tent. Dusk closed into a dirty night. The wind increased to blow harder than at any time of the day or previous night. It made the rain come in fierce rattling spasms, nearly horizontal. I believe half a gale was blowing outside. It made a great noise round the barn, and several times flung open the door of the loft, which we did not seem able to jam successfully.

A boy came, very kindly in the rough and pitch-black weather, to bring us some candles. He said it was jolly brave to have come in that boat. He did not think we would get away on the next day. We had told those who had asked that we had come round from Eigg. She was a good sea-boat; yes, there was a biggish swell outside – that sort of conversation. When we had talked a little the boy said: "I guess I'll hae to be makin' tracks". That must have been one of the travelling cinema's visits to Portree or Mallaig.

The Tuesday evening was probably the best part of the trip. The roaring fire made the loft like an oven and the wind buffeting and moaning outside only emphasised the cosiness inside. We got our clothes dried again. Hugh and I were dog-tired, but well fed and warm and dry; the day's work had been the hardest either of us had ever done. It was sheer pleasure to relax in the warmth, to savour the tiredness of the body. It is accepted that the pleasures of holiday are often keenest either in retrospect from another season as a distillation of the best, or as airy plans for the future before being brought down by reality. It was true even of this gala Tuesday nearly passed. I could not say that it had been enjoyed; we had been too busy and occupied with other thoughts. But now the sleepy evening allowed us conscious enjoyment of the very moment. The tension was relaxed. We could say, "Well, we have done it". Then go on to say how much more easily we could have done it, if we had started the day with the experience of the day. The boat business had been clumsy, but it was difficult to see how else we could have managed, with the lack of anchorages, given that degree of bad weather and requiring a boat of heavy seaworthiness.

We thought we should probably be stormbound in Canna over the next day. Stormbound or not, a comfortable, a legal exploration of Canna would make several good days. However, now that the stag was killed, the next urgency was to hurry its head to a taxidermist before it went bad. We must go if we could.

The Canna barn is well placed, standing a little back from the eastern shore, by a small bay; very fine for bathing in the right weather. Pigs live under the loft. Corn marigolds, which are very showy, grow nearby. The barn was used as the headquarters of the Glasgow University Expedition to Canna, 1936 – a group of biologists; they had left the straw which made such ease in the loft. The northern universities commonly adopt various of the Western Isles to 'do' them with such expeditions. Disregarding the high-sounding scientific research – which is natural history, though specialised – they make good holidays and are free, being paid for by university grants. It was a pity that with these good quarters, a boat for cruising and the island to explore, we had to think of leaving Canna early the next morning.

When we could stay awake no longer we fell asleep in the straw. We had so overheated the loft with the great fire that the ventilating rat holes in the door were quite welcome.

Chapter Seven

Wednesday

The sea was obviously worse than on Tuesday and the wind stronger, though perhaps the latter had lost some of Tuesday evening's viciousness. It had moved a little into the north. We decided to put out, to have a look at the sea at any rate, then turn back if it was too bad.

The draught through the rat holes had been very searching in the small hours. We lit the fire for warmth to eat by, and to cheer the packing up. At seven in the morning it was cold even in the sun; another loath parting with night warmth and sleep. The sun alternated with rain squalls. The early light lit slantwise on the corn marigolds, while they yielded with the oat swathes to the blast.

We took two old sacks we had found in the boat and wrapped the stag's head in them, making an awkward parcel. There was nobody about. We damped down the fire and brushed out the loft and carried the gear down to the jetty. We had come in the evening before at near high water and the boat was dry now but the tide was flowing and would soon float her. While it approached we filled the fuel tanks and looked over the motor, cleaned its plugs, topped up its oil and baled out the night's rain. When required the engine started easily; we let it run in neutral to warm up while we rowed out clear of the shore seaweed. Strong wind through the rigging always seems to me solid. It parts itself on the rigging, as wire parts cheese and as it is cleaved, it whines.

One of the Scandinavian mackerel ships (the type as once served by our present boat) was moored in the harbour. We motored past it, past the steamer, out of shelter and into the open sea.

After that came the four and a half anxious hours between Canna and Point of Sleat; John at the tiller throughout. They began with an exact cross-sea – the swell came round the north coast of Canna with the north-west wind behind it. This was very tricky, but we had only once or twice to slew round to face the seas head-on. Canna, our late refuge, was soon only visible from the top of the swell. At other times we were in a small and private world; the trough of the swell, a bowl of rushing and powerful water, surrounded by a skyline of sea. As soon as we had cleared the land we met a different, confused sea. This was the meeting of the new north-west swell from the north coast of Canna and the old south-west swell coming up through the Sound of Canna, that is, between Canna and Rum. It was not possible to keep to a definite course for an hour or so.

We shipped a fair amount of water, but not to the stage of embarrassment as the bilge pump was adequate. This pump was not engine driven; it was a rotary hand pump with the handle under one gunwale. To prime it you had to fish up the rubber pipe which sucked from the bilges and fill it with sea water gathered in a gym-shoe, for want of a better receptacle, then plunge the pipe back into the bilge water without causing an airlock. The bilge water was corrupted with old black, engine oil and sludge and it was black in colour, however much fresh water came over the side to leaven it.

The engine was apparently comfortable – its fiendish clatter had been accepted as normal – but it became very warm. The cylinder head nuts bubbled, as a crab out of water blows a little froth of bubbles from the opening of its gill chamber. It is a phenomenon sometimes disquietly remarked upon in an old car engine, particularly when overheated. But the gearbox was my worry. From the hole at the top of the casting where the gear change lever joined the insides trailed a slime of hot brown oil, which increased as the gearbox became hotter. Nothing further happened however and you could always bear your hand on the gearbox. I always worry about engines.

We kept well off the coast of Rum. The spray was flung high there, and hung in curtains that seemed slowly to disintegrate and resolve again into sea-water. A patch of pale sunlight found the coast, as we tossed a mile offshore and the surf and broken water fairly sparkled. The streams coming down the north-west coast were bright metallic squiggles across the land, as if scribbled by a pencil; a pencil mark on paper has that same metallic bright lustre when the sun takes it in a certain way. The north-west swell drove straight into Kilmory Bay, smashing on the rocks and sand and the wind took away the spindrift. Any sort of boat drawn up there would have been immovably stormbound; we were lucky to have got away on Tuesday night. For a few minutes now and then the high ground of Skye showed in the north but for the most part it was hidden in a bad weather pall. In the clearer patches Point of Sleat showed some miles ahead.

By the time we were opposite Kilmory the conflicting swells had resolved themselves into a big following sea, high and fast. A following sea is the most comfortable of all, they say, until it becomes dangerous, which it soon does. We were pooped about four times, and once, unpleasantly, flung sideways, but recovered before the next wave. John shouted how unpleasant it was to have water swirling green round his bottom; and how sore, from continual shifting to ease the hardness of wet board. Small boat sailors know that sore, wet hardness so very well. There was always the sensation peculiar to a following sea: you surf-ride on the crest – a fine surge forward – then the boat seems to hang, the motor still revving, but there is no progress. It is as if the clutch were slipping. The white crest races on ahead and above and you hang until picked up by the next one. Sometimes the crest broke in its white smother alongside, sometimes ahead or astern; you looked back to see the swell tops running after you. The water swilled in now and then, but though the gunwale was often under, the decking kept most of the water out. We should have been pumping continuously without that decking; the product of somebody else's hire money. Rain squalls kept coming up behind. One in particular burst around us with such force that momentarily the swell and broken water were eased. This one made the sea seem to boil, and a layer of steam rose from it. It cloaked visibility with a grey curtain in every direction; an extraordinary desolate prospect. Always the swell tops ran against the sky. The few shearwaters that manoeuvred low over the waters banked vertically in the air, wings board-stiff, as they crossed our bows.

Canna slowly closed behind Rum. Eigg opened beyond the corner of Rum, the two islands gradually stood apart. For a short time Muck showed between them, beyond the Sound of Rum, down in the south. Point of Sleat was clear ahead and slowly nearing and it was a great relief to get round it. We gave a wide berth to its black rocks and confused surf, then, instead of setting straight for Mallaig, turned in under the lee of Skye, to check the fuel and oil and to change drivers. John was tired after nearly five hours at the tiller. He had had no chance to relax all that time from the kick of the tiller and the wearying strain of watching every wave.

It is a pity that photographs of rough seas never look rough. The one or two photographs we'd taken flattened the seas disappointingly. The enterprise in general had not been covered by photographs though Hugh had carried a little camera and was continually popping it off; the results were certainly documentary. Photography might almost be an index of a holiday; the fewer the photographs, the more memorable the time and the more action.

We headed across to the Mainland on the last lap. The swell still followed but greatly diminished. We crossed with the mailboat on the outward trip, pitching steeply even there in the Sound of Sleat; she would soon be getting very wet. She was the only craft besides ourselves which was out. The seas were empty.

The six new red and white houses on the hillside by Mallaig were a good landmark and showed brightly when the sun shone. The broken sea was blue and green and white; grey in the squalls. Approaching Mallaig we had to return to the main concern – the stag and associated circumstances, these having been forgotten for the past seven hours. We had simply to hope that nobody would notice the awkward armful, which would have to be carried ashore in broad daylight; no artifice could cover its passage from boat to car. We came round the iron cage on that rock off Mallaig harbour, round the steamer pier and the fishing boats along their quay, past the *Ossianic*, to ground on the sand, beyond which, via a few yards of littered old cans, fish-bones, orange skins and similar harvest of the seas, is the main street. At any rate the police were not waiting for, "a small white motor boat, probably heading for Mallaig".

Hugh and I walked straight up to fetch our cars. Spoilt young men I'm afraid, with a sports car each, but I hope redeemed by the disrepair of the cars as well as the owners. We argued with the garage where the proprietor has a monopoly. Two shillings a night he said. We protested at the London charges which we felt were excessive for small car in tin shed. "I know my charges," said the proprietor, several times. High feeling. Profiteering in Mallaig. We drove the cars down to the shore and unloaded the boat into them. There were only two or three small boys watching as the bad weather kept the quays and street clear of people. The moment came to transfer the stag's head. We draped the parcel with a couple of ground-sheets to hide its shape, John handed it to me from the boat. I hurried it up the beach and pushed it under the car's hood. The small boys were not very interested.

We cleaned the boat as best we could, wiped off some of the oil slime, tied her up fore and aft, and left her. Mr MacY was not in his general store so we drove up the hill to his house, stopping at the post office to send a telegram: 'Completely Successful', to Mr MacX, who had taken a fatherly interest. We paid Mr MacY for the boat on behalf of her owner, and added a bit for a good sea-boat and for some paint scraped off on Canna jetty. We had come from Canna, we said.

"In that small boat! Well then," he said, "You had a nairve, yes, you had a nairve." This was a rich compliment.

It was good to be free of Mallaig, and to be off the sea, which, even now, from the height of the road, looked white-flecked and unkind as far as the eye could see. That had certainly been the riskiest part of the trip, if not the most nerve-wracking. Rum was in the sun, at the end of the green and white sea.

The fine spell had not only broken up, it was also the end of the Scottish summer. This wind would carry off the first of the autumn leaves, although it was still August. One horse chestnut was already yellowed. Some of the beech boles were thick with lichen (due to the west coast sopping wetness) but others were so clean, light grey and smooth, scrubbed by the full force of wind and rain, that they were the texture of young ash poles. Both might have been a different species from the south country's chalk-grown beeches. The foliage was wind bitten and of a dying yellowness, as of disease; not to be compared with the slow ripening of southern leaves. But it was good to see any trees growing to size up there. The rowans were more fitting, heavy with wind-turned fruit.

The middle part – the bad stretch – of the Mallaig road took one and a quarter hours; 14 miles in 75 minutes = 11 1/5 mph. We stopped short of Fort William to sort out our goods and repack the cars, because Hugh was going elsewhere in Scotland, by previous arrangement, for the second week of his holiday. John and I were going home, as soon as we had disposed of the stag's head in Glasgow. The rifle, having done what was required of it, was packed back into its original case ready to be returned by rail to the London gunmakers who had hired it out. The Mallaig road seemed quite easy; success and the end of the trip were the right moods for it.

We had some drinks in Fort William and then parted. Well, goodbye Hugh, goodbye John, goodbye Robert; we'll all meet in London. John and I drove on south. Streaming rain began at once and went on all night. By half past ten we had reached Loch Lomond, and on those banks we found a place to pull off the road and to put up the tent in the pouring darkness.

Chapter Eight

Thursday

It had rained so hard overnight that the grass stood in pools of water; we pushed the wet tent into the back of the car and got under the hood. It was only thirty odd miles to Glasgow. We stopped at the first telephone box we came to on the outskirts of the town, and looked up 'Taxidermists' in the Classified Telephone Directory Business & Professional. There was only one. From Sauchiehall Street we found his place of business. It was a large dingy Victorian private house, with steps and a knocker and a brass plate, in a drab backstreet.

We unpacked the stag's head in the hall. It seemed wrong so to expose it, quite openly and in the light of day, to foreign eyes. No-one besides ourselves had hitherto seen it or known of its existence. And one felt diffident in displaying and accepting as valuable, this piece of dead meat; particularly out of place in the environment of hall carpet and hatstand. What odd merchandise the business world can deal in. The head looked unhappy in the cement dust from the sacks, its eyes dusted over. The man did not appear to think much of it, but asked no questions and was thus told no lies.

I must say that our stag was a proper stag, not just a buck; that is to say he had passed his apprenticeship by the stages: knobber, brocket, spayed and staggard to stag. He had come of age. He was five years old and had four points – brow, bay, très and the top one to each antler. The head had just begun to smell, although only about forty hours dead. We had been so familiar with it as a travelling companion and as master factor in our doings, that it had seemed much longer than forty hours; it was almost a pity to leave it. Yet it was really a relief finally to be parted from the head since it was an exacting master.

From the taxidermist and the head, we went in search of breakfast, and landed in a blowsy cafe at the end of the street. A scratchy gramophone was 'Doin' the Lambeth Walk'; coffee came from its bottle. And here, in these untasteful surroundings, the Rum expedition may be said to have ended.

Chapter Nine

Later

The head of course is now mounted on an oak shield. But it is ill-stuffed and I think it will soon moulder. However, it looks distinguished enough and you are not allowed to hang hats on its antlers. The silver plate says cryptically: 'Kilmory 1938'.

The expedition has had no repercussions whatever; we did not hear even the slightest rumour, although Hugh and I were in Mallaig the following year. We never heard whether the owner really did come to his island that Tuesday. I often wondered if the headless corpse was ever found; the skeleton would be clean and white by now.

The same moral arguments remained after, as before, the expedition's fruition. I wondered one or twice, though as an academic point, whether this deer-stealing was in fact plain stealing. A gesture was hardly a gesture if no-one saw it. The other side, of course, still said that perfect poaching was not only undiscovered, it was not even suspected. But the moral issues of poaching, whether for sport or reward or gesture for-private-circulation-only are open to discussion, and will remain so as long as game

83

preservation remains. I can't say they now seem very interesting.

But I should like, before closing, to make an observation on the unreality and other faults of adventure stories. The Rum enterprise might in some ways be described as an adventure, and therefore, when written up, as an adventure story. As such it shows that fictional adventure stories must remain fictional; they cannot happen or be put into reality. They are like plans that have never been proved by practice. The difficulties that stop us in practice are not thought of, the happy coincidence does not coincide; in short, things do not go according to plan. Look at the Rum expedition – luck all the way; luck with the boat, with the authorities, stalking luck, luck with the weather just allowing sea operations; precious little useful planning, difficulties somehow neutralised as encountered and helped out with luck. It was 'All Right on the Night', after all.

More than this, the pleasant excitement of adventure stories is replaced by the unpleasant nervous tension of adventures. The real pleasure of adventures comes when they are safely over; the more frightening or uncomfortable, the happier they are in retrospect.

A last point is that all sorts of illegal and antisocial activities, such as murder, are applauded in fiction; but not, of course, in fact. This shows the immorality and untruth-fulness of fiction; the argument that it is only imaginary, is false, because fiction is required to be plausible.

In our small case I admit that the apostrophe to Rum was full of holes, but the answer to the decadence of modern youth, ill-chosen use of leisure, the machine age etc is that that leisure produced the hardest day's work of our lives. Also, of course, you have to remember that we boys were only young once.

Moral

A summing-up gives this brief moral. 'You Are Instructed To Keep Off The Grass'. 'Trespassers Will Be Prosecuted'. 'No Admittance Except On Business'. The indication is sufficiently obvious. Your only reason for touching is because the notice says: 'Do Not Touch'.

That's the only point. The few days of Scottish August left a good memory of hostile bare country, dirty weather, cold, rough sea, big game and nervousness. It was a good trip you know. That was the day's result; neither satisfaction nor shame, as I said. I offered this report disinterestedly, as a practical experience. Also I might just mention that, for a time, another result was a mood of friendly familiarity whenever one came on a pub called 'The Stag's Head'.

THE END